Today's Creative Crock-Pot® Slow Cooker Cookbook

Today's Creative
CROCK-POT®
Slow Cooker Cookbook

Robin Taylor Swatt

Pascoe Publishing, Inc.
Rocklin, California

The nutritional analyses are based on typical serving sizes and optional ingredients have not been included.

Cover design by Kayla Blanco
Page design by Kayla Blanco

Published in the United States by:

Pascoe Publishing, Inc.
Rocklin, California
www.pascoepublishing.com

ISBN: 978-1-929862-76-4

Library of Congress Control Number: 2001093205

09   10   11   12

10   9   8   7   6   5   4   3

Printed in China

TABLE OF CONTENTS

ACKNOWLEDGMENTS

Thank you to my wonderful family – Jeff, Eli, and Vivian – who helped me with the testing of these recipes and gave me valuable feedback. Much appreciation also goes out to my extended family and friends who also served as taste testers during this book's creation. Truly, this book was a community effort.

–Robin Taylor Swatt

INTRODUCTION

When *The New Creative Crock-Pot® Slow Cooker Cookbook* was first published in 2001, I was completely unprepared for the enthusiastic and delighted response I received from so many busy cooks across the nation. Many people quickly labeled this book as the "go to" cookbook for easy-to-prepare and delicious family meals.

Today, our lives revolve even faster around work, sports and family activities, so I've included in this revised edition new recipes to suit your on-the-go lifestyle. Inside these pages, you'll find satisfying one-dish recipes, recipes with added fresh ingredients, and new global specialties using flavorful spices and fresh herbs. You'll also find tempting Crock-Pot® slow cooker appetizers, desserts, snacks and sauces. And, for the busiest days of all, I've included a little treasury of "5 + 5" recipes using your Crock-Pot® slow cooker, 5 ingredients and 5 minutes or less of prep time. Enticing home-cooked meals don't get any easier than that!

I hope you savor all of the recipes in this cookbook and every moment spent sharing them with your family. These recipes are a gift to your family from mine…for the way we live today.

— Robin Taylor Swatt

CHAPTER ONE
Crock-Pot® Slow Cooker
Hints & Tips

1. *Stirring*
Unless a recipe specifically instructs, you won't need to stir foods while cooking in your Crock-Pot® slow cooker. In fact, taking the lid off to stir food causes the Crock-Pot® slow cooker to lose a significant amount of heat, extending the cooking time required.

2. *Adding Ingredients at the End of the Cooking Time*
Certain ingredients should be added toward the end of the cooking time. These include:
   ‣ Milk and sour cream. Add during the last 15 minutes of cooking time.
   ‣ Seafood. Add in the last hour of cooking time, unless the recipe specifies otherwise.

3. *Increasing the Recipes*
Most of these recipes and those on the Crock-Pot® slow cooker website (www.crockpot.com) can be increased. For best results, follow these guidelines:
   ‣ Herbs and spices are flavor-intensive and should only be increased by half again when doubling the recipe.

➤ When preparing soup or a stew, you may double all ingredients except liquids, seasonings and herbs. Increase the liquid by half or as needed and do not double ingredients used to thicken the soup or stew. Use additional amounts only as needed.

➤ For roasts and stews, place the vegetables in the stoneware and add the meat. Add the liquid after adding the meat.

4. *Vegetables*

➤ Most vegetables should be thinly sliced or placed near the sides or bottom of the stoneware.

➤ You may double or triple vegetable recipes as desired. Increase any herbs or spices by 25 percent and increase any liquids by half.

5. *Rice*

For best results, use long grain converted rice or a specialty rice as the recipe suggests. If the rice is not cooked completely after the suggested time, add an extra 1 to 1½ cups of liquid per cup of cooked rice and continue cooking for 20 to 30 minutes.

6. *Pasta*

For best results, first partially cook the pasta in a pot of boiling water until just tender. Add the pasta to the Crock-Pot® slow cooker during the last 30 minutes of cook time.

7. *Beans*

It is best to boil dried beans (navy, white, pinto, etc.) before cooking them in the Crock-Pot® slow cooker. Cook the beans in water on the stovetop per package directions until tender, drain, and add them to the recipe as instructed.

8. *Frozen Foods*

You can cook frozen meat in your Crock-Pot® slow cooker without first thawing the meat, however use the following tips for success:

➤ Add at least 1 cup of warm liquid to the stoneware before placing the meat in the stoneware.

➤ Do not preheat the unit.

➤ Cook recipes containing frozen meats for an additional 4 to 6 hours on Low or 2 hours on High.

9. *Cooking Temperatures and Food Safety*

Cooking meats in your Crock-Pot® slow cooker is perfectly safe. According the U.S. Department of Agriculture, bacteria in food is killed at a temperature of 165°F. Meats cooked in the Crock-Pot® slow cooker reach temperatures higher than that and then plateau at 209°F during the slow cooking process. It is important to follow the recommended cooking times and to the keep the cover on your Crock-Pot® slow cooker closed during the entire cooking process.

10. *Removable Stoneware*

The removable stoneware in your Crock-Pot® slow cooker makes it easy to prep food ahead of time and also makes cleaning a snap. Follow the owner's instructions included with your Crock-Pot® slow cooker and note the following:

> ‣ To cook food that has been refrigerated in the stoneware, place the stoneware on the heating base and turn the temperature control to the desired setting. The bowl and food do not need to warm to room temperature before heating. Use the maximum cooking time and continue cooking, if needed, until the meat is tender and cooked through.
> ‣ Do not preheat the slow cooker.
> ‣ Serve hot drinks and appetizers directly from your Crock-Pot® slow cooker. Select the Warm heat setting to maintain the proper serving temperature.

11. *Browning Meat*

Due to the nature of slow cooking, meat does not brown as it would if cooked in a skillet or oven. It is not necessary to brown meat before slow cooking, however, if you prefer the appearance and enhanced flavors of browned meat, sauté your meat in a skillet with a little oil, then place the meat in the stoneware and follow the recipe as usual.

12. *Breads and Cakes*

You'll have delicious results by following these hints:

> ‣ Do not over-beat breads and cakes. Follow all recommended mixing times.
> ‣ Do not add water to the slow cooker unless the recipe instructs you to do so.
> ‣ Do not double or triple the ingredients for baked goods or cheesecakes. For best results, repeat the recipe as needed to increase the quantity of servings.
> ‣ After the bread or cake has cooked, allow to cool for 5 to 10 minutes before removing from the stoneware.

Chapter Two

Savory Sauces, Appetizers & Sides

SMOKY ARTICHOKE CHEESE DIP

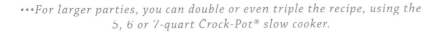

makes 15 servings

This easy dip is the quintessential party favorite! Your guests will compete for the last spoonful, so serve with plenty of sourdough bread rounds or crackers.

8 oz.	mozzarella cheese, shredded
1 cup	Parmesan cheese, grated
1 cup	mayonnaise (substitute lowfat, if desired)
1 cup	canned artichoke hearts, drained and chopped
½ cup	roasted red peppers, finely chopped
4 oz. can	diced fire-roasted green chiles
2 cloves	garlic, minced
½ tsp.	salt
¼ tsp.	freshly ground black pepper
	cooking spray

•••*For larger parties, you can double or even triple the recipe, using the 5, 6 or 7-quart Crock-Pot® slow cooker.*

Coat the stoneware with cooking spray and add all of the ingredients. Mix thoroughly.   Cover and cook in the Crock-Pot® slow cooker on High for about 1½ hours.

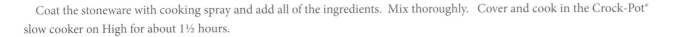

GREEN CHILE CORN DIP

makes 15 servings

This simple appetizer is a perfect prelude to a Southwest-inspired feast. Serve with white or blue corn tortilla chips.

1 lb.	Jack cheese, shredded
1 cup	Parmesan cheese, shredded
1 cup	mayonnaise (substitute lowfat, if desired)
½ cup	canned creamed corn
½ cup	fresh or frozen corn kernels
4 oz. can	diced green chilies
2 cloves	garlic, minced
1 Tbs.	red pepper flakes
1 Tbs.	sun-dried tomatoes, reconstituted and finely chopped
	cooking spray

•••*For larger parties, you can double or even triple the recipe, using the
5, 6 or 7-quart Crock-Pot® slow cooker.*

Coat the stoneware with cooking spray. Add all ingredients to the Crock-Pot® slow cooker and mix thoroughly. Cover; cook on High for 1 hour.

Bacon & Broccoli Cheese Spread

Cook on High
1 hour

makes 15 servings

Bacon, broccoli and cheddar cheese create a classic flavor combination. This recipe takes those flavors and creates a gold medal winner.

10¾ oz. can	condensed cream of mushroom soup
¼ cup	water
½ tsp.	dry mustard
8 slices	smoked bacon, cooked until crisp and crumbled
2 cups	broccoli florets, blanched and chopped
3 cups	cheddar cheese, shredded

•••*For larger parties, you can double or even triple the recipe, using the 5, 6 or 7-quart Crock-Pot® slow cooker.*

In a small bowl, whisk together the soup, water and dry mustard. Place the bacon, broccoli and cheese in the Crock-Pot® slow cooker and add the soup mixture. Stir well until combined. Cover; cook on High for 1 hour. Serve with sourdough rounds or crispy breadsticks.

COOK ON HIGH
1 HOUR

CREAMY SPINACH DIP

makes 15 servings

Serve this warm dip in the Crock-Pot® slow cooker or ladled into a sourdough bread bowl. Arrange raw vegetables, your favorite crackers or sourdough bread slices around the dip.

12 oz.	cream cheese, cubed
½ cup	heavy whipping cream
10 oz.	frozen chopped spinach, squeezed dry
1 oz. pkg.	dehydrated onion soup mix
1 tsp.	prepared hot sauce
½ cup	green onions, finely sliced
1 tsp.	fresh lemon juice

•••*For larger parties, you can double or even triple the recipe, using the 5, 6 or 7-quart Crock-Pot® slow cooker.*

Combine the cream cheese and whipping cream in the Crock-Pot® slow cooker. Cover and heat on High until the cheese is melted, about 30 minutes. Add the spinach, soup mix and hot sauce, and stir thoroughly. Cover; cook on High for 30 minutes. Shortly before serving, add the green onions and lemon juice and mix thoroughly again.

CLASSIC CHEESE FONDUE

serves 12 as an appetizer or 6 as an entreé

COOK ON HIGH
1 HOUR & LOW
2 HOURS

Dip beef, chicken, vegetables or cubes of artisan bread into this delicious fondue. Kirsch, a specialized brandy distilled from cherry juice, adds a hint of intense flavor and is available in grocery stores.

2½ cups	dry white wine
3 cloves	garlic, finely minced
16 oz.	Gruyère cheese, grated
1 lb.	Swiss cheese, grated
3 Tbs.	flour
3 Tbs.	Kirsch liqueur
¼ tsp.	ground nutmeg

•••To increase this recipe, double all ingredients and use a 5, 6 or 7-quart Crock-Pot® slow cooker.

In a large saucepan, heat the wine and garlic to a simmer. Combine the Gruyère and Swiss cheese with the flour in a large bowl and slowly add the cheese mixture to the wine. Stir constantly until the cheeses are completely integrated and melted. Add the Kirsch and stir. Pour the fondue into the Crock-Pot® slow cooker and sprinkle with the nutmeg. Cover; cook on High for 1 hour. Stir the fondue, replace the cover and cook on Low for 2 hours.

COOK ON HIGH
30 MINUTES

HOT CRAB DIP

makes 12 servings

This seafood starter is a tasty way to kick off a party. The richness of the crab and cheese is enhanced by the bright flavors of lemon and chives. Serve with potato chips for crunch.

12 oz.	cream cheese, cubed
¼ cup	heavy whipping cream
1 cup	Parmesan cheese, grated
2 6½ oz. cans	lump crab meat
1 oz. pkg.	dehydrated onion soup mix
1 Tbs.	Worcestershire sauce
2 cloves	garlic, minced
1 tsp.	fresh lemon juice
	salt to taste
	fresh chives, minced, for garnish

•••*For larger parties, you can double or even triple the recipe, using the 5, 6 or 7-quart Crock-Pot® slow cooker.*

Combine the cream cheese and whipping cream in the Crock-Pot® slow cooker. Cover and heat on High until the cheese is melted, about 45 minutes. Add the Parmesan cheese, crab meat, onion soup mix, Worcestershire sauce, and garlic and stir thoroughly. Cover; cook on High for 30 minutes. Shortly before serving, add the lemon juice and mix thoroughly. Salt to taste. Sprinkle the top with fresh minced chives as a garnish.

Arizona Black Bean Dip

Cook on High
1½ to 2 hours

makes 10 servings

This Southwest-inspired dip gets a boost with the addition of fresh goat cheese. The pumpkin seeds as garnish also give the dip a nice crunch. Serve with your favorite tortilla chips.

2 14 oz. cans	black beans, drained
1 medium	onion, finely diced
4 cloves	garlic, minced
1 Tbs.	ground cumin
1 tsp.	cayenne pepper
14 oz.	fresh goat cheese, crumbled (or any other fresh farmer's cheese)
¼ cup	green onions, thinly sliced (reserve 1 Tbs. for garnish)
¼ cup	fresh cilantro, chopped (reserve 1 Tbs. for garnish)
2 Tbs.	pumpkin seeds, shelled and toasted, for garnish

•••*For larger parties, you can double or even triple the recipe, using the 5, 6 or 7-quart Crock-Pot® slow cooker.*

Combine all the ingredients in the Crock-Pot® slow cooker, except for the garnish ingredients. Cook on High 1½ to 2 hours, or until the cheese has melted and is bubbly. Transfer to a serving dish and garnish with a sprinkling of green onions, cilantro and pumpkin seeds.

ASIAN SPICED CHICKEN WINGS

COOK ON LOW
5 TO 6 HOURS

makes 6 servings

Chicken wings are always crowd pleasers. Serve with plenty of napkins and cucumber slices.

3 lbs.	chicken wings
½ cup	soy sauce
½ cup	dark brown sugar, packed
¼ cup	ketchup
1 Tbs.	dry sherry
2 tsp.	fresh ginger, minced
2 cloves	garlic, minced
¼ cup	hoisin sauce
1 Tbs.	fresh lime juice

•••*To increase this recipe, increase the chicken wings to 5 pounds and use a
5, 6 or 7 quart Crock-Pot® slow cooker. All other ingredients remain as listed.*

Pat the chicken wings with paper towels until dry. Broil the chicken wings for 10 minutes on each side, or until browned. Transfer the chicken wings to the Crock-Pot® slow cooker. In a small bowl, combine the soy sauce, brown sugar, ketchup, sherry, ginger and garlic. Drizzle over the chicken wings and toss to coat. Cover; cook on Low 5 to 6 hours (or on High for 2 to 3 hours).

Remove the wings from the stoneware, place on a serving platter, and reserve ¼ cup of the juices in the Crock-Pot® slow cooker. Discard the remaining juices. Combine the reserved juice with the hoisin sauce and lime juice. Stir to blend and drizzle the sauce over the chicken wings.

ZESTY ITALIAN BARBECUE MEATBALLS

COOK ON LOW
4 HOURS

makes about 40 meatballs

Fresh homemade meatballs are superior, but if you're really pressed for time, use the frozen meatballs available at your local grocery store. Serve the meatballs with cocktail picks.

Meatballs:

2 lbs.	lean ground beef
1 medium	yellow onion, finely chopped
1 cup	dried bread crumbs
¼ cup	fresh Italian parsley, minced
2 cloves	garlic, minced
½ tsp.	freshly ground black pepper
½ tsp.	dry mustard
2	eggs, beaten

Sauce:

1½ cups	bottled barbecue sauce
¾ cup	tomato paste
⅓ cup	ketchup
⅓ cup	brown sugar, packed
½ cup	water, as needed
1 tsp.	liquid smoke

•••You may double the meatball ingredients for the 5, 6 or 7-quart Crock-Pot® slow cooker, but do not increase the sauce ingredients.

In a mixing bowl, combine the meatball ingredients. Form into walnut-sized balls. Bake the meatballs in a shallow baking dish at 350°F for 20 minutes or until browned. Drain off any fat. Transfer the meatballs to the Crock-Pot® slow cooker. In a separate mixing bowl, combine the sauce ingredients and mix thoroughly. Pour the sauce over the meatballs and stir lightly. Cover; cook on Low for 4 hours (or on High for 2 hours). Stir once in the middle of cooking to baste the meatballs with sauce. Remove the meatballs from the sauce to serve.

COOK ON LOW
6 TO 8 HOURS

TWO-STEP SWEET & SOUR MEATBALLS

makes 20 servings

It couldn't get any easier to make a scrumptious hors d'oeuvre! Using prepared meatballs cuts your prep time into mere minutes.

32 oz.	prepared frozen meatballs
1 cup	tomato sauce
20 oz. can	crushed pineapple, with juice
¼ cup	brown sugar, packed
¼ cup	apple cider vinegar

Place the meatballs in the Crock-Pot® slow cooker. Mix together the remaining ingredients and pour over the meatballs, stirring to combine. Cover; cook on Low 6 to 8 hours (or on High for 3 to 4 hours).

ISLANDER CHICKEN DRUMSTICKS

Makes 12 appetizer or 6 entrée servings

COOK ON LOW
4 TO 6 HOURS

Serve with plenty of napkins to capture the sweet, tangy sauce from these drumsticks.

¾ cup	apricot-pineapple jam
2 Tbs.	soy sauce
1 tsp.	ground ginger
1 tsp.	lemon zest, grated
3 lbs.	chicken drumsticks
¾ cup	canned pineapple wedges, drained

•••*To increase this recipe, double all ingredients and use a 5, 6 or 7-quart Crock-Pot® slow cooker.*

In a small mixing bowl, combine the jam, soy sauce, ginger and lemon zest. Dip each drumstick into this mixture and place into the Crock-Pot® slow cooker. Pour the remaining jam mixture over the drumsticks. Add the pineapple chunks and mix thoroughly. Cover; cook on Low 4 to 6 hours (or on High for 2 to 3 hours). Remove the drumsticks and pineapple from the stoneware and place on a broiling tray. Broil for 10 minutes or until the chicken has browned.

Mango Spiced Cocktail Ribs

makes 12 to 15 servings

Mango chutney adds piquant sweetness to these fall-off-the-bone beef ribs. Serve with plenty of napkins!

3 lbs.	beef short ribs
1 cup	mango chutney
1 clove	garlic, minced
1 Tbs.	curry powder
½ tsp.	ground cinnamon
½ tsp.	salt

•••*To increase this recipe, double the ingredients and use the
5, 6 or 7-quart Crock-Pot® slow cooker.*

In a large skillet, brown the short ribs. Pour off the excess fat. In a small bowl, combine the chutney, garlic, curry powder, cinnamon and salt. Rub the mixture over the ribs and place the ribs in the Crock-Pot® slow cooker. Drizzle any remaining chutney mixture over the ribs. Cover; cook on low for 6 to 8 hours (or on High for 3 to 4 hours).

Easy Barbecue Ribs

makes 8 servings

Savory ribs perfect for game day!

3 lbs.	beef or pork spareribs, sliced into serving pieces
1 tsp.	salt
1 tsp.	freshly ground black pepper
1	medium onion, sliced
14 oz.	bottle of your favorite barbecue sauce
1 Tbs.	brown sugar
2 Tbs.	fresh lemon juice

•••*To increase this recipe, double the ingredients and use the 5, 6 or 7-quart Crock-Pot® slow cooker.*

Rub the spareribs with salt and pepper and broil for 15 minutes until browned. Place the spareribs and onion into the Crock-Pot® slow cooker. Combine the barbecue sauce, sugar, and lemon juice and pour over the ribs. Cover; cook on Low 8 to 10 hours (or on High for 4 to 5 hours).

COOK ON LOW
4 HOURS

FRESH VEGETABLE PAELLA

serves 4 as an entrée or 6 as a side dish

This side dish is a twist on the Spanish classic. You may also serve this as a main vegetarian entrée.

5 oz.	frozen chopped spinach, thawed and drained
2 cups	converted white rice
4 cups	vegetable broth
1	green bell pepper, seeded and chopped
1 medium	tomato, sliced into wedges
1 medium	onion, chopped
1 medium	carrot, diced
3 cloves	garlic, minced
1 Tbs.	fresh Italian parsley, minced
1 tsp.	saffron threads
1 tsp.	salt
½ tsp.	freshly ground black pepper
13¾ oz. can	artichoke hearts, quartered, rinsed and well-drained
½ cup	frozen petite peas

•••*To increase this recipe, double the ingredients and use the
5, 6 or 7-quart Crock-Pot® slow cooker.*

Combine the spinach, rice, vegetable broth, green pepper, tomato, onion, carrot, garlic, parsley, saffron, salt, and black pepper in the Crock-Pot® slow cooker. Mix thoroughly. Cover; cook on Low 4 hours (or on High for 2 hours). Add the artichoke hearts and peas to the paella 15 minutes prior to serving. Mix thoroughly to combine, cover and continue cooking until heated through.

CREAMY CURRIED SPINACH

COOK ON LOW
3 TO 4 HOURS

makes 6 to 8 servings

The cream and butter of this recipe balance the intense flavoring imparted by the curry and garlic.

3 10 oz. pkgs.	frozen spinach, thawed and drained
1 large	yellow onion, chopped
4 cloves	garlic, minced
2 Tbs.	curry powder
2 Tbs.	butter or margarine, melted
¼ cup	chicken broth
¼ cup	heavy cream
1 tsp.	lemon juice

•••*To increase this recipe, double all ingredients except the broth and cream.*
Use the 5, 6 or 7-quart Crock-Pot® slow cooker.

Combine the spinach, onion, garlic, curry powder, butter, and chicken broth in the Crock-Pot® slow cooker. Cover; cook on Low 3 to 4 hours (or on High for 2 hours). Thirty minutes before the end of the cooking time, add the heavy cream and lemon juice. Mix to combine, cover and heat through.

COOK ON LOW
8 TO 10 HOURS

SLOW-ROASTED TOMATO & GARLIC SAUCE

makes 8 cups

Serve with pasta dishes, chicken, rice, beans or fish. Double the recipe and freeze the sauce to enjoy fresh tomato flavors all year-round.

15 medium	Roma tomatoes, cores removed
1 large	yellow or white onion, roughly chopped
7 cloves	garlic, peeled
½ cup	fresh basil, chopped
2 tsp.	dried crushed oregano
¼ cup	extra-virgin olive oil
1½ Tbs.	sugar
1 tsp.	salt
½ tsp.	freshly ground black pepper

•••*To increase this recipe, double all the ingredients except the oil and use the 6 or 7-quart Crock-Pot® Slow Cooker.*

Place the tomatoes, onion and garlic in the Crock-Pot® slow cooker. In a small bowl, whisk together the basil, oregano, oil, sugar, salt and pepper. Drizzle over all and toss lightly. Cover; cook on Low 8 to 10 hours (or on High for 4 to 5 hours).

Working in batches if necessary, spoon the sauce into a blender and process until the sauce is slightly chunky or as desired. (Alternately, use a potato masher to create a chunky consistency.) Repeat with the remaining sauce. Adjust seasonings with salt and pepper to taste. Use while warm or freeze in airtight containers until needed.

SUMMER VEGETABLE RATATOUILLE

Cook on Low
4 to 6 hours

makes 4 servings

This southern French classic is the perfect way to use abundant, fresh summer vegetables.

2 medium	eggplant, cut into ½-inch slices
	salt
1 large	white onion, chopped
3 cloves	garlic, minced
2 medium	zucchini, cut into ½-inch slices
1	red pepper, seeded and chopped
1 medium	yellow squash, cleaned and cut into ½-inch pieces
2 medium	tomatoes, sliced into wedges
¼ cup	extra-virgin olive oil
¼ cup	dry white wine
1 Tbs.	sugar
1 Tbs.	red wine vinegar
¼ cup	Parmesan cheese, grated

*•••To increase this recipe, double all ingredients, except the olive oil and wine.
Use the 5, 6 or 7-quart Crock-Pot® slow cooker.*

Place the eggplant slices in a large colander and sprinkle with salt to remove excess water. After 30 minutes, wash the salt off the eggplant and pat dry with a paper towel. In a large skillet, lightly sauté the eggplant, onion, garlic, zucchini, and red pepper.

Place the vegetables in the Crock-Pot® slow cooker and add the squash, tomatoes, olive oil, wine, sugar and vinegar. Cover; cook on Low 4 to 6 hours (or on High for 2 to 3 hours). Sprinkle with Parmesan cheese before serving.

GOLDEN ROASTED ROOT VEGETABLES

COOK ON LOW
6 TO 8 HOURS

makes 6 side servings

A great winter dish of hearty, warm flavors.

2 large	parsnips, peeled and cut into ½-inch pieces
4 large	carrots, peeled and cut into ½-inch pieces
6 medium	Yukon Gold potatoes, peeled and cut into ½-inch pieces
1 Tbs.	fresh tarragon, minced
1 Tbs.	fresh sage, minced
¼ cup	butter, melted
½ tsp.	salt
½ tsp.	freshly ground black pepper
1 tsp.	dark brown sugar

•••*To increase this recipe, double the ingredients and use the
5, 6 or 7-quart Crock-Pot® slow cooker.*

Combine all of the ingredients in the Crock-Pot® slow cooker. Thoroughly coat the vegetables with the herbs, seasonings and butter, stirring well to combine. Cover; cook on Low 6 to 8 hours (or on High for 3 to 4 hours).

GLAZED GINGERED CARROTS

makes 8 to 10 servings

COOK ON LOW
6 TO 8 HOURS

Simply tangy, wholesome carrots!

32 oz. pkg.	whole baby carrots
¼ cup	honey
3 Tbs.	apple juice
1½ Tbs.	fresh ginger, grated
½ tsp.	kosher salt
2 Tbs.	fresh parsley, finely chopped

•••*To increase this recipe, double the ingredients and use the
5, 6 or 7-quart Crock-Pot® slow cooker.*

Place the carrots in the Crock-Pot® slow cooker. In a small bowl, whisk together the honey, apple juice, ginger and salt. Pour over the carrots and toss to coat evenly. Cover; cook on Low for 6 to 8 hours (or on High for 3 to 4 hours). Toss with the fresh parsley before serving.

CORN AND CHEESE CHOWDER

COOK ON LOW
6 TO 9 HOURS

makes 6 servings

This creamy soup is an excellent centerpiece for a delicious family dinner.
Just serve with crusty French bread and a tossed green salad, and the meal is complete.

1	large onion, finely chopped
1 clove	garlic, minced
1 Tbs.	vegetable oil
2 tsp.	cumin seed
3 cups	chicken broth
2	medium potatoes, peeled and chopped
1 cup	canned creamed corn
2 cups	fresh or frozen corn kernels
¼ cup	fresh Italian parsley, chopped
1 cup	cheddar cheese, grated
13 oz. can	evaporated milk
2 Tbs.	fresh chives, chopped

•••*To increase this recipe, double all ingredients except the evaporated milk.*
Increase the evaporated milk to 19 ounces and use the 5, 6 or 7 quart Crock-Pot® slow cooker.

In a small skillet, sauté the onion and garlic in the oil until golden. Drain and place in the Crock-Pot® slow cooker. Add the remaining ingredients, except for the cheddar cheese, evaporated milk and chives. Mix thoroughly. Cover; cook on Low 6 to 9 hours (or on High for 2 to 4 hours) or until the potatoes are tender. Add the cheese and evaporated milk during the last hour of cooking and garnish with chives before serving.

STUFFED CABBAGE LEAVES

makes 4 servings

A popular recipe around the world, this easy dish combines interesting flavors with a fun presentation.

1 lb.	lean ground beef
½ cup	cooked white or brown rice
1 tsp.	salt
½ tsp.	freshly ground black pepper
2 tsp.	fresh thyme, minced
2 tsp.	fresh Italian parsley, minced
¼ tsp.	ground nutmeg
¼ tsp.	ground cinnamon
12	large cabbage leaves, blanched until pliable
6 oz. can	tomato paste
¾ cup	dry white wine

•••*To increase this recipe, double all ingredients except the tomato paste and white wine. Use the 5, 6 or 7 quart Crock-Pot® slow cooker.*

In a mixing bowl, combine the all the ingredients, except for the cabbage leaves, tomato paste and white wine. Place 2 tablespoons of the meat mixture in each cabbage leaf and roll to form a package. Place each roll into the Crock-Pot® slow cooker. In a small mixing bowl, whisk together the tomato paste and white wine. Pour over the cabbage rolls. Cover; cook on Low 8 to 10 hours (or on High for 4 to 5 hours).

Frijoles "Refritos"

makes 8 to 10 servings

Spanish for "refried beans," these frijoles are the perfect accompaniment for any Latin-inspired meal!

1 lb.	dried pinto beans, soaked in water for at least 8 hours and then drained
¼ lb.	salt pork
4 cups	water
1 medium	yellow onion, finely chopped
2 cloves	garlic, minced
2 Tbs.	canola oil
2 tsp.	kosher salt

•••*To increase this recipe, double all ingredients and use a 6 or 7-quart Crock-Pot® slow cooker.*

Place the beans, salt pork, and water in the Crock-Pot® slow cooker. Cover; cook on Low for 8 to 10 hours. Remove the salt pork and discard. Drain the beans and reserve the cooking liquid.

In a large saucepan, sauté the onion in the oil on medium heat until the onion is translucent, about 7 minutes. Add the garlic and stir until fragrant, about 5 minutes. Add the cooked beans and mash, using a potato masher or a fork, until the beans are smooth with only a few whole beans remaining. Add the reserved cooking liquid a spoonful at a time until the beans are smooth and reach the desired consistency.

COOK ON HIGH
2 HOURS

ITALIAN MUSHROOM RISOTTO WITH PEAS

makes 8 servings

The typical risotto recipe requires constant attention and stirring. This recipe combines all of the ingredients and your Crock-Pot® slow cooker takes care of the rest. The result is a creamy, delectable side dish!

1 medium	yellow onion, finely chopped
3 Tbs.	extra-virgin olive oil
2 cups	crimini mushrooms, sliced
¼ cup	dried porcini mushrooms, reconstituted, cleaned, and chopped
1¼ cups	arborio rice
¼ cup	dry white wine
3¼ cups	vegetable or chicken broth
1 tsp.	salt
½ cup	Parmesan cheese, grated
½ cup	frozen peas, thawed

•••*To increase this recipe, double the ingredients and use the
5, 6 or 7-quart Crock-Pot® slow cooker.*

In a medium saucepan, sauté the onion in the olive oil over medium heat until translucent. Add the crimini mushrooms and cook until the mushrooms have softened and the liquid has evaporated. Place the mushroom mixture in the Crock-Pot® slow cooker and add the porcini mushrooms, rice, wine, broth, and salt. Stir to combine. Cover; cook on High for 2 hours or until all the liquid is absorbed. In the final 5 minutes of cooking, add the cheese and peas, mixing lightly to combine. Serve immediately.

THYME & BASIL HERBED RICE

COOK ON MED.
4½ HOURS

makes 6 to 8 servings

Plain rice is elevated by the use of fresh, savory herbs and buttery chicken broth. Add cooked slices of lean chicken, beef or pork just before serving to create a one-dish dinner for a hungry crowd.

1 medium	yellow onion, finely chopped
2 Tbs.	extra-virgin olive oil
2 cups	long grain white rice
4¼ cups	chicken broth
1 tsp.	kosher salt
1 Tbs.	fresh flat-leaf parsley, finely chopped
1 Tbs.	fresh basil, finely chopped
1 tsp.	thyme leaves, chopped

Sauté the onion in the olive oil in a small saucepan, stirring and cooking until the onion is soft, about 7 minutes. Spoon the onion into the Crock-Pot® slow cooker and add the rice, broth, and salt, mixing to combine. Cover; cook on Medium for 4½ hours (or on High for 2¼ hours). Before serving, toss the rice with the parsley, basil and thyme. Serve while warm.

COOK ON MED.
4½ HOURS

RED MEXICAN RICE

makes 8 servings

Also known as "Spanish Rice," this classic accompaniment to a Mexican entrée is often paired with Frijoles Refritos *(see P. 35).*
Easy to prepare and beautifully colored, with just a slight spiciness from the jalapeño pepper.

1 medium	yellow onion, finely chopped
2 Tbs.	vegetable oil
2 cloves	garlic, minced
2 cups	long grain white rice
2 cups	tomato sauce
2¼ cups	chicken broth
1 Tbs.	fresh cilantro, finely chopped
1 tsp.	kosher salt
1	jalapeño pepper, sliced in half lengthwise and seeded

•••*To increase this recipe, double the ingredients and use the*
5, 6 or 7-quart Crock-Pot® slow cooker.

In a medium saucepan over medium heat, sauté the onion in the oil until translucent and soft, about 7 minutes. Add the garlic and cook until fragrant, about 30 seconds. Add the rice and cook, stirring lightly, until the rice turns opaque, about 5 minutes. Place the rice mixture in the Crock-Pot® slow cooker and add the remaining ingredients. Cover; cook on Medium for 4½ hours (or on High for 2¼ hours). Before serving, remove the pepper halves.

Sweet Potato Gratin

makes 6 servings

Unlike many sweet potato dishes, this gratin relies on the inherent sweetness of the potato itself. The end result is an earthy flavor with the added citrus freshness of orange.

4 to 6 medium	sweet potatoes, peeled and sliced into 1-inch pieces
2 Tbs.	orange juice
1 Tbs.	orange zest
¼ cup	dark brown sugar, packed
1 tsp.	ground cinnamon
½ tsp.	kosher salt
	cooking spray

•••To increase this recipe, double the ingredients and use the 5, 6 or 7-quart Crock-Pot® slow cooker.

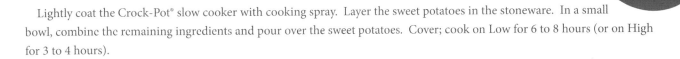

Lightly coat the Crock-Pot® slow cooker with cooking spray. Layer the sweet potatoes in the stoneware. In a small bowl, combine the remaining ingredients and pour over the sweet potatoes. Cover; cook on Low for 6 to 8 hours (or on High for 3 to 4 hours).

COOK ON LOW
8 TO 10 HOURS

COUNTRY SCALLOPED POTATOES WITH HAM

makes 6 servings

Smoky ham pairs well with the creamy potatoes for a homestyle feast.
To serve as an entrée, increase the smoked ham to ½ pound of cubed pieces or slices.

4 large	potatoes, peeled and thinly sliced
1 tsp.	freshly ground black pepper
1 tsp.	salt
2 cups	medium cheddar cheese, shredded
1 large	yellow onion, thinly sliced
12 thin slices	country smoked ham
¼ cup	fresh Italian parsley, minced
1 cup	half-and-half cream
½ cup	butter, melted
½ tsp.	ground paprika
	cooking spray

•••*To increase this recipe, double all ingredients except the milk and butter.*
Use the 5, 6 or 7-quart Crock-Pot® slow cooker.

Lightly coat the stoneware with cooking spray. Layer one-fourth of the potato slices in the Crock-Pot® slow cooker. Season with salt and pepper to taste. Top with ¼ cup cheddar cheese, one-fourth of the onion slices and 2 slices of the ham. Continue layering until four layers of potatoes, cheese, onion and ham are created. In a small bowl, combine the parsley, cream, butter, paprika and remaining pepper and salt. Pour the sauce over the layers without mixing or altering the layers. Cover; cook on Low for 8 to 10 hours (or on High for 4 to 5 hours).

ROSEMARY RED JACKET POTATOES

COOK ON LOW
6 TO 8 HOURS

makes 8 side servings

An elegant accompaniment to beef or lamb.

10 to 12 medium	red potatoes, cut into quarters
¼ cup	fresh lemon juice
⅛ cup	butter or margarine, melted
1 Tbs.	extra-virgin olive oil
3 cloves	garlic, minced
2 Tbs.	fresh rosemary leaves, minced
¾ tsp.	salt
½ tsp.	ground paprika
¼ cup	fresh Italian parsley, chopped

•••*To increase this recipe, double the ingredients and use the
5, 6 or 7-quart Crock-Pot® slow cooker.*

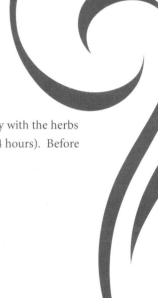

Combine all of the ingredients except the parsley in the Crock-Pot® slow cooker. Coat the potatoes evenly with the herbs and seasonings, turning with a large spoon to combine. Cover; cook on Low 6 to 8 hours (or on High 3 to 4 hours). Before serving, toss the potatoes with the fresh parsley for added flavor and color.

COOK ON LOW
6 TO 8 HOURS

CORNBREAD & SAUSAGE STUFFING

makes 6 to 8 servings

Free up your oven for the main course by creating this luscious stuffing in your Crock-Pot® slow cooker. You won't believe how moist and well-seasoned this side dish is...and neither will your friends and family!

1 lb.	bulk sausage filling
1 medium	onion, chopped
2 ribs	celery, sliced
1 Tbs.	canola oil
3	eggs, beaten
1 loaf	cornbread (8-inch size), cubed
8 slices	day-old bread, toasted and cubed
10¾ oz. can	condensed cream of chicken soup
2½ cups	chicken broth
1 tsp.	poultry seasoning

•••*To increase this recipe, double the ingredients and use the 5, 6 or 7-quart Crock-Pot® slow cooker.*

In a medium saucepan, sauté the sausage, onion, and celery in the canola oil, until the sausage has browned and the onion is translucent. Drain off the fat. Place the sausage mixture and the remaining ingredients in the Crock-Pot® slow cooker, mixing to combine well. Cover; cook on Low for 6 to 8 hours.

CREAMY PARMESAN POLENTA

COOK ON LOW
6 TO 8 HOURS

makes 6 to 8 servings

A traditional polenta takes time and effort. This easy recipe takes only a few minutes of prep time. Serve while warm or cool and cut into triangles before serving. Add a twist by brushing the polenta lightly with olive oil and grilling over medium heat just prior to serving.

2 Tbs.	butter, melted
6 cups	boiling water
2 cups	yellow cornmeal
2 tsp.	kosher salt
1 tsp.	freshly ground black pepper
1 cup	Parmesan cheese, grated
	cooking spray

Coat the Crock-Pot® slow cooker with cooking spray. Place the melted butter, boiling water, cornmeal, salt and pepper in the stoneware, whisking to combine until all of the cornmeal lumps are gone and the mixture is smooth. Cover; cook on Low for 6 to 8 hours (or on High 3 to 4 hours). Just prior to serving, add the cheese and mix well. Serve immediately.

BRUNCH FLORENTINE

makes 4 to 6 breakfast servings

Similar to a hearty frittata, this layered breakfast will be welcomed by family and friends.

1½ cups	cheddar cheese, grated and divided
9 oz. pkg.	frozen spinach, thawed and drained
1 cup	white bread, cubed
1 cup	fresh button mushrooms, sliced
½ cup	green onions, thinly sliced
6	eggs
1½ cups	milk
½ cup	heavy cream
1 tsp.	salt
1 tsp.	freshly ground black pepper
1 tsp.	garlic powder
	cooking spray

•••*To increase this recipe, double all ingredients and use a
5, 6 or 7-quart Crock-Pot® slow cooker.*

Lightly coat the stoneware with cooking spray. Scatter half of the cheese in the bottom of the Crock-Pot® slow cooker and layer the spinach, bread, mushrooms and green onions over the cheese. In a medium mixing bowl, whisk together the eggs, milk, cream, salt, pepper and garlic powder until thoroughly combined. Pour the egg batter over the layered mixture. Do not stir or mix. Sprinkle the remaining cheese over the top. Cover; cook on High 1½ to 2 hours.

HEARTY CHEESE HASH BROWNS

COOK ON LOW
6 TO 8 HOURS

makes 6 to 8 servings

Transform this side dish to a farmer's breakfast by adding 1½ cups diced ham or cooked, shredded chicken breast.

5 cups	frozen hash brown potatoes
2 cups	cheddar cheese, grated
1 cup	milk
½ cup	half-and-half cream
½ cup	green onions, thinly sliced
1 cup	frozen peas
1 tsp.	salt
1 tsp.	freshly ground black pepper
1 tsp.	ground paprika

•••*To increase this recipe, double all ingredients and use a
5, 6 or 7-quart Crock-Pot® slow cooker.*

Combine all ingredients in the Crock-Pot® slow cooker and mix thoroughly. Cover; cook on Low 6 to 8 hours (or on High for 3 to 4 hours).

SMOKED SAUSAGE WITH CABBAGE & APPLES

makes 6 servings

COOK ON LOW
6 TO 8 HOURS

1½ lbs.	smoked sausage, cut into 2-inch pieces
3	cooking apples, thickly sliced
½ head	red cabbage, shredded
1	medium onion, sliced
½ cup	brown sugar
1 tsp.	salt
½ tsp.	freshly ground black pepper
½ cup	apple juice

•••*To increase this recipe, double all ingredients and use a 5, 6 or 7-quart Crock-Pot® slow cooker.*

Layer the sausage, apples, cabbage and onion in the Crock-Pot® slow cooker in the order listed above. Sprinkle the brown sugar, salt, and black pepper on top. Pour the apple juice over all the other ingredients. Do not stir. Cover; cook on Low 6 to 8 hours (or on High for 3 to 4 hours).

COOK ON LOW
6 TO 8 HOURS

EASY ITALIAN SAUSAGE SCRAMBLE

makes 6 servings

Choose your favorite style of Italian sausage to make this dish memorable or opt for an extra spicy sausage to add a flavor boost.

1 medium	yellow onion, diced
1½ lbs.	Italian sausage, removed from casing
6 medium	red potatoes, diced
1 medium	tomato, diced
1 cup	fresh or frozen kernel corn
¼ cup	fresh Italian parsley, minced
2 cups	cheddar cheese, grated
1 cup	milk
1½ tsp.	salt
2 tsp.	freshly ground black pepper

•••*To increase this recipe, double all ingredients and use a 5, 6 or 7-quart Crock-Pot® slow cooker.*

In a medium skillet, sauté the onion and brown and crumble the sausage. Drain off any fat and transfer the sausage and onions to the Crock-Pot® slow cooker. Add the remaining ingredients, mixing well to combine thoroughly. Cover; cook on Low for 6 to 8 hours (or on High for 3 to 4 hours), or until the potatoes are tender.

MIGAS

COOK ON LOW
4 TO 6 HOURS

makes 6 servings

A classic Southwestern breakfast, packed with lively flavors. Serve with corn tortillas and refried beans for an authentic touch.

6 large	eggs, beaten
½ cup	green onions, thinly sliced
½ cup	red bell pepper, diced
1 cup	Jack cheese, grated
1 cup	medium cheddar cheese, grated
¾ cup	mild salsa
1 tsp.	ground cumin
1 tsp.	garlic powder
1 tsp.	dried oregano
¾ cup	milk
2½ cups	salted tortilla chips, slightly broken

*•••To increase this recipe, double all ingredients and use a
5, 6 or 7-quart Crock-Pot® slow cooker.*

Combine all the ingredients in the Crock-Pot® slow cooker. Mix thoroughly. Cover; cook on Low 4 to 6 hours (or on High for 2 to 3 hours).

FRESH VEGETABLE & THREE CHEESE FRITTATA

makes 6 servings

Full of fresh vegetables, this Italian-style breakfast dish is a great alternative for vegetarians. Round out the meal with toast, fresh fruit, and steaming cups of Italian espresso.

1 cup	zucchini, thinly sliced
1 cup	yellow squash, thinly sliced
½ cup	red pepper, seeded and diced
2 cloves	garlic, minced
1 cup	asparagus, cut into 1-inch pieces
8 large	eggs, beaten
½ cup	fontina cheese, grated
½ cup	mozzarella cheese, grated
½ cup	Parmesan cheese, grated
¼ cup	fresh Italian parsley, minced
1 tsp.	salt
1 tsp.	freshly ground black pepper

•••*To increase this recipe, double all ingredients and use a
5, 6 or 7-quart Crock-Pot® slow cooker.*

In a medium skillet, sauté the zucchini, yellow squash, red pepper and garlic until tender. Transfer the vegetables to the Crock-Pot® slow cooker and add the remaining ingredients, mixing thoroughly to combine. Cover; cook on Low 4 to 6 hours (or on High for 2 to 3 hours).

CHAPTER THREE

Hearty Beef, Pork & Lamb Entrées

Wild Mushroom Beef Stew

makes 5 servings

This classic beef stew is given a twist with the addition of flavorful shiitake mushrooms. If shiitake mushrooms are unavailable in your local grocery store, you can substitute other mushrooms of your choice.

1½ to 2 lbs.	beef stew meat, cut in 1-inch cubes
⅛ cup	flour
½ tsp.	salt
½ tsp.	black pepper
1½ cups	beef broth
1 tsp.	Worcestershire sauce
1 clove	garlic, minced
1	bay leaf
1 tsp.	ground paprika
4	shiitake mushrooms, sliced
2 medium	carrots, sliced
2 medium	potatoes, diced
1 small	white onion, chopped
1 rib	celery, sliced

•••To increase this recipe, double the meat, mushrooms, carrots, potatoes, onion and celery and use the 5, 6 or 7-quart Crock-Pot® slow cooker.

Put the beef in the Crock-Pot® slow cooker. Mix together the flour, salt and pepper, and sprinkle over the meat; stirring to coat each piece of meat with flour. Add the remaining ingredients and stir to mix well. Cover; cook on Low 10 to 12 hours (or on High for 4 to 6 hours). Remove the bay leaf and stir the stew thoroughly before serving.

Sunday Dinner Beef Roast

makes 10 to 12 servings

COOK ON LOW
10 TO 12 HOURS

Slow cooking creates a tender, rich roast beef that will wow your guests. You can make the meal even more elegant by using new potatoes, baby carrots and pearl onions instead of cut-up vegetables.

3 to 4 lbs.	rump, pot, or chuck roast
2 cloves	garlic, sliced
1 tsp.	freshly ground pepper
1 tsp.	salt
½ cup	white wine
3 medium	potatoes, chopped
2 large	carrots, sliced
1	yellow onion, chopped
1 tsp.	fresh parsley, minced
1 tsp.	fresh rosemary, leaves only
1 tsp.	fresh thyme, minced

•••*To increase this recipe, prepare a 5 to 7 lb. roast and doubt the amount of seasonings, potatoes and onion. Use a 5, 6 or 7-quart Crock-Pot® slow cooker.*

Using a small knife, make several slits all over the roast. Insert slices of garlic into each slit. Rub the outside of the roast with the salt and pepper. Place in the Crock-Pot® slow cooker and add the remaining ingredients. Cover; cook on Low 10 to 12 hours (or on High for 5 to 6 hours). Remove the roast and let it rest for 15 minutes before slicing.

ITALIAN-STYLE ROAST

COOK ON LOW
8 TO 10 HOURS

makes 6 servings

Accented by traditional Italian herbs and flavorings, this succulent roast is drizzled with a rich tomato sauce and is best served over rice or pasta.

6 oz. can	tomato paste
2 cloves	garlic, minced
1 oz. pkg.	dehydrated onion soup mix
2 tsp.	fresh oregano, chopped
2 tsp.	fresh thyme, chopped
1 tsp.	salt
1 tsp.	freshly ground black pepper
2 lbs.	chuck roast, trimmed of any excess fat
16 oz. can	whole tomatoes, drained and chopped
1 medium	yellow onion, chopped
2 medium	carrots, chopped
1 medium	russet potato, chopped
1 large	celery rib, sliced
2 whole	bay leaves

*•••To increase this recipe, double all ingredients and use a
5, 6 or 7-quart Crock-Pot® slow cooker.*

In a small mixing bowl, combine the tomato paste, garlic, onion soup mix, oregano, thyme, salt and pepper. Rub this mixture all over the chuck roast and place the roast in the Crock-Pot® slow cooker. Add the remaining ingredients and any leftover tomato sauce. Cover; cook on Low 8 to 10 hours (or on High for 4 to 5 hours). Remove the bay leaves before serving.

COOK ON LOW
4 TO 6 HOURS

FRENCH BEEF BURGUNDY

makes 6 servings

This rustic French dish is chock full of substantial flavor. The beef becomes "fall-apart tender," so serve with crusty French bread or over mashed potatoes to capture the juices.

½ lb.	bacon, diced
¼ cup	all-purpose flour
½ tsp.	salt
½ tsp.	freshly ground black pepper
2 lbs.	boneless beef chuck, cut into 1-inch cubes
1 cup	burgundy wine
½ cup	beef broth
1½ cups	frozen peeled pearl onions
3 medium	carrots, cut into 1-inch pieces
8 large	white mushrooms, sliced in half
3 cloves	fresh garlic, sliced
2	bay leaves
¼ cup	fresh parsley, minced

*•••To increase this recipe, double all ingredients and use a
5, 6 or 7-quart Crock-Pot® slow cooker.*

In a medium skillet, cook the diced bacon until the fat has rendered and the bacon is crispy. Remove the bacon and set aside. Combine the flour, salt and black pepper. Dredge the beef cubes in the flour mixture and brown in the bacon fat in the same skillet. Discard the remaining fat and spoon the beef into the Crock-Pot® slow cooker. Deglaze the skillet with the wine and beef broth by bringing the liquids to a boil. Scrape up any browned bits.

Place the liquid, bacon, onions, carrots, mushrooms, garlic, and bay leaves into the stoneware with the beef and mix thoroughly to combine. Cover; cook on Low 4 to 6 hours (or on High for 2 to 3 hours). Skim off any fat that has risen to the top and remove the bay leaves. Before serving, add the parsley and mix to combine.

BEEF & SHIITAKE MUSHROOM STROGANOFF

COOK ON LOW
8 TO 10 HOURS

makes 8 servings

Using rich, earthy shiitake mushrooms, this dish becomes a sophisticated twist on traditional stroganoff.
Serve over hot, cooked egg noodles or rice.

2 lbs.	London broil beef, cut into thin strips
¼ cup	all-purpose flour
½ tsp.	salt
½ tsp.	freshly ground black pepper
2 medium	yellow onions, thinly sliced
4 oz.	shiitake mushrooms, cleaned, woody stems removed, caps sliced
4 oz.	crimini mushrooms, cleaned and sliced
1½ cups	beef broth
½ cup	dry white wine
1 tsp.	Worcestershire sauce
1½ cups	sour cream
12 oz.	egg noodles, cooked and drained
2 Tbs.	fresh parsley, minced

•••*To increase this recipe, double all ingredients except the beef broth and white wine.*
Use the 5, 6 or 7-quart Crock-Pot® slow cooker.

Dredge the beef strips in the flour, salt, and pepper. Place the coated beef strips in the Crock-Pot® slow cooker. Add the onions, mushrooms, beef broth, wine, and Worcestershire sauce. Cover; cook on Low 8 to 10 hours (or on High 4 to 5 hours). Add the sour cream to the stroganoff. Mix well and cook for another 5 minutes on High. Spoon over the egg noodles to serve and garnish with the parsley.

COOK ON LOW
8 TO 10 HOURS

CLASSIC BEEF BRISKET

makes 4 servings

A typically tough cut of beef becomes succulent and rich!

4 medium	red potatoes, roughly chopped
2 medium	carrots, roughly chopped
1 medium	white onion, roughly chopped
2 lbs.	beef brisket, unseasoned and trimmed of fat
½ tsp.	salt
½ tsp.	freshly ground pepper
½ tsp.	smoked paprika
½ cup	beef broth
2 Tbs.	all purpose flour
	dash of gravy seasoning (such as Kitchen Bouquet™)

•••*To increase this recipe, double all ingredients and use a*
5, 6 or 7-quart Crock-Pot® slow cooker.

Place the potatoes, carrots, and onion in the Crock-Pot® slow cooker. Season the brisket with salt, pepper, and paprika and place on top of the vegetables. Cut the brisket in half if necessary to fit into the stoneware. Cover; cook on Low for 8 to 10 hours.

Remove the brisket and vegetables. Pour the broth into a small saucepan. In a small bowl, whisk together 2 tablespoons flour with 3 tablespoons of reserved broth. Bring the broth in the saucepan to a boil and add the flour mixture slowly, whisking to incorporate. Reduce to a simmer. Add a dash of the gravy seasoning, and salt and pepper to taste. Heat until the gravy has thickened.

Slice the brisket thinly against the grain and place on a serving platter with the vegetables. Pour the gravy over the brisket slices and vegetables.

PICADILLO

makes 6 servings

COOK ON LOW
6 TO 8 HOURS

*Latin American picadillo is a breeze to make with your favorite enchilada sauce.
Serve as a filling for tacos or burritos, or spoon this simple entrée over rice.*

2½ to 3 lbs.	chuck roast, trimmed of fat
28 oz. can	mild enchilada sauce
4 oz. can	chopped green chilies
1 large	yellow onion, finely chopped

•••*To increase this recipe, double all ingredients except the
enchilada sauce. Use the 5, 6 or 7-quart Crock-Pot® slow cooker.*

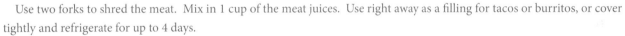

Place the chuck roast in the Crock-Pot® slow cooker. Top with the enchilada sauce, green chilies, and onion. Cover; cook on Low 6 to 8 hours (or on High 3 to 4 hours). When done, remove the chuck roast and cool on a large rimmed platter. Reserve the meat juices.

Use two forks to shred the meat. Mix in 1 cup of the meat juices. Use right away as a filling for tacos or burritos, or cover tightly and refrigerate for up to 4 days.

COOK ON LOW
8 TO 10 HOURS

BEER-BRAISED BEEF SHORT RIBS

makes 6 servings

Short ribs become oh-so-tender when slow cooked with a stout beer in this delightful recipe.

¼ cup	all-purpose flour
½ tsp.	kosher salt
½ tsp.	freshly ground black pepper
½ tsp.	smoked paprika
½ tsp.	dried mustard
2½ lbs.	beef short ribs
2 Tbs.	extra-virgin olive oil
1 large	onion, sliced
2 cloves	garlic, minced
12 oz.	bottle full-bodied beer
2 Tbs.	flour
3 Tbs.	cold water

•••*To increase this recipe, double all ingredients except the beer. Add 18 oz. beer
as directed above and use the 5, 6 or 7-quart Crock-Pot® slow cooker.*

Combine the flour, salt, black pepper, paprika, and dried mustard. Dredge the short ribs in the flour mixture and brown in the olive oil in a medium skillet. Place the onions and garlic in the Crock-Pot® slow cooker and top with the browned ribs. Pour the beer over the ribs. Cover; cook on Low 8 to 10 hours (or on High for 4 to 6 hours).

Remove the ribs and onion and place on a serving platter. Cover with aluminum foil to keep warm. In a small bowl, whisk together the flour and water and add to the juices in the stoneware. Set to High and heat and stir until the juices thicken into a gravy. Pour the gravy over the short ribs and serve.

Spinach & Feta-Stuffed Meatloaf

Cook on Low
8 to 10 hours

makes 8 servings

Kick up the flavor with this spinach and feta-stuffed meatloaf.

2 lbs.	ground beef
2 large	eggs
⅔ cup	seasoned bread crumbs
1 oz. pkg.	dry onion soup mix
2 cloves	garlic, minced
¼ cup	Parmesan cheese, grated
½ cup	ketchup, divided
¾ cup	feta cheese, crumbled
3 Tbs.	sun-dried tomatoes, minced
10 oz. pkg.	frozen chopped spinach, thawed and squeezed dry

•••*To increase this recipe, use 3 eggs and ¾ cup ketchup. Double all remaining ingredients. Use a 5, 6 or 7-quart Crock-Pot® slow cooker.*

In a large bowl, combine the ground beef, eggs, bread crumbs, onion soup mix, garlic, Parmesan cheese and all but 2 tablespoons of the ketchup. In a small bowl, mix together the feta cheese and sun-dried tomatoes. On a cutting board covered with wax paper, pat the meat mixture into a rectangle, approximately 6 inches by 10 inches.

Spread the feta cheese mixture over the meat rectangle to within 1-inch of the edges. Place the spinach over the feta. Using the wax paper, roll the meat loaf so that the meat completely covers the cheese and spinach center and seal tightly. Make sure that the ends of the meat loaf are also completely sealed. Place in the Crock-Pot® slow cooker, on one end, if necessary. Top with the remaining ketchup. Cover; cook on Low 8 to 10 hours (or on High for 4 to 6 hours).

COOK ON LOW
6 TO 8 HOURS

FAVORITE BEEF CHILI

makes 8 servings

This chili is full of warm, layered flavors, but has no beans – a must for chili purists. However, add a can of pinto or black beans for added protein, if desired, and serve with cornbread or tortilla chips.

1 large	yellow onion, finely chopped
2 Tbs.	extra-virgin olive oil
½ lb.	bulk sausage
2 lbs.	lean ground beef
8 oz. can	tomato paste
1 clove	garlic, minced
1 Tbs.	ground cumin
1 Tbs.	chili powder
1 tsp.	dried mustard
1 tsp.	dried oregano
1½ tsp.	kosher salt
1 tsp.	freshly ground black pepper
28 oz. can	chopped tomatoes, drained

•••*To increase this recipe, double all ingredients and use a
5, 6 or 7-quart Crock-Pot® slow cooker.*

In a large skillet, cook the onion in the olive oil over medium-low heat, stirring until softened, about 8 minutes. Add the sausage and beef and cook over medium-high heat, until the meats are well-browned. Drain off any fat. Place the meat mixture in the Crock-Pot® slow cooker and add the remaining ingredients. Stir to combine well. Cover; cook on Low for 6 to 8 hours (or on High for 3 to 4 hours).

STUFFED CHEDDAR MEATLOAF

COOK ON LOW
6 TO 8 HOURS

makes 6 servings

A classic combination of meatloaf ingredients with a tomato and cheese twist!

1½ lbs.	extra-lean ground beef
2 cups	soft bread crumbs
1 cup	ketchup
½ cup	yellow onion, chopped
2 eggs	beaten
1 tsp.	salt
1 tsp.	freshly ground black pepper
8 slices	cheddar or American cheese, each cut into 2 strips
2 Tbs.	tomato paste

•••*To increase this recipe, double all ingredients and use the 5, 6 or 7-quart Crock-Pot® slow cooker.*

In a large mixing bowl, combine all of the ingredients except the cheese and tomato paste. Shape half of the meat mixture into a loaf. Arrange 8 cheese strips on top of the meat and cover the cheese with the remaining meat mixture, pressing the edges together to seal.

Place the filled meatloaf in the Crock-Pot® slow cooker and cover with the tomato paste. Top the tomato paste with the remaining cheese slices. Cover; cook on Low 6 to 8 hours (or on High for 3 to 4 hours).

COOK ON LOW
8 TO 10 HOURS

TERIYAKI BEEF SALAD

makes 4 servings

A light and intensely flavorful salad entrée. Serve with warm, crusty bread for a perfect summer evening meal.

1 lb.	beef flank steak, visible fat removed
3 Tbs.	soy sauce
2 Tbs.	canola oil
2 Tbs.	honey
2 Tbs.	garlic, finely chopped
1 tsp.	ground ginger
2 Tbs.	green onions, chopped
10 cups	romaine lettuce greens, washed and torn
1 cup	cherry tomatoes, halved
1	cucumber, peeled and thinly sliced
2 ribs	celery, washed and diced
¼ tsp.	freshly ground black pepper

•••*To increase this recipe, double all ingredients and use a
5, 6 or 7-quart Crock-Pot® slow cooker.*

Place the steak in the Crock-Pot® slow cooker (cut in half, if necessary, to fit). In a small bowl, combine the soy sauce, oil, honey, garlic, ground ginger and green onions. Mix well and pour over the steak. Cover and cook on Low for 8 to 10 hours (or on High for 3 to 4 hours.) Transfer the steak to a carving platter and slice the steak thinly across the grain of the meat. Reserve the marinade.

To assemble the salad, toss the lettuce, tomatoes, cucumber and celery in a large serving bowl. Place the beef slices on top of the salad, drizzle with the warm marinade and toss again. Divide the salad onto individual plates, dust each salad with black pepper and serve immediately.

ANY DAY OF THE WEEK BEEF CHILI

COOK ON LOW
6 TO 8 HOURS

makes 6 to 8 servings

Deliciously spicy, this chili's heat quotient can be increased by the addition of cayenne pepper to taste and canned green chilies.

2 medium	yellow onions, chopped
4 cloves	garlic, minced
2	green bell peppers, chopped
1 Tbs.	extra-virgin olive oil
2 lbs.	ground chuck beef
2 14 oz. cans	pinto beans, drained
14 oz. can	tomatoes, drained and chopped
4 oz. can	green chilies, chopped
1 Tbs.	dried oregano
2 tsp.	ground cumin
1 tsp.	cayenne pepper (or to taste)
1 tsp.	freshly ground black pepper
1 tsp.	salt
1 cup	beef or chicken broth
1 cup	sour cream, for garnish
1 cup	sharp cheddar cheese, grated, for garnish
2 Tbs.	green onions, thinly sliced, for garnish

•••*To increase this recipe, double all ingredients and use a 5, 6 or 7-quart Crock-Pot® slow cooker.*

In a large skillet, sauté the onions, garlic, and bell peppers in the oil until soft. Add the ground beef and brown. Drain off any excess fat. Transfer the meat and vegetables to the Crock-Pot® slow cooker. Add the remaining ingredients except the garnishes, and mix thoroughly. Cover; cook on Low 6 to 8 hours (or on High for 3 to 4 hours.). To serve, offer the sour cream, cheese and green onions at the table.

COOK ON LOW
8 TO 10 HOURS

TANGERINE BROCCOLI BEEF

makes 6 servings

Tender beef meets vegetables and tangerines in a tangy Asian sauce.

1½ lbs.	boneless beef top sirloin steak, cut into thin strips
1	red bell pepper, seeded and sliced into strips
2 cloves	garlic, minced
1 Tbs.	fresh ginger, grated
¼ tsp.	crushed red pepper
1 Tbs.	soy sauce
2 Tbs.	rice vinegar
1 Tbs.	oyster sauce
¼ cup	dry sherry
2 cups	broccoli flowerets
1½ Tbs.	cornstarch
2 Tbs.	water
2 11 oz. cans	mandarin orange segments, drained
½ cup	green onions, thinly sliced
4 cups	sticky white rice (substitute brown or white rice)

···*To increase this recipe, double all ingredients and use a
5, 6 or 7-quart Crock-Pot® slow cooker.*

Combine the steak, bell pepper, garlic, ginger, red pepper, soy sauce, rice vinegar, oyster sauce and sherry in the Crock-Pot® slow cooker. Cover; cook on Low 8 to 10 hours (or on High for 4 to 5 hours). Thirty minutes before serving, add the broccoli flowerets and mix to combine. Combine the cornstarch and water in a small bowl and add to the juices in the stoneware. (This will thicken the juices to make the sauce.) Replace the cover and finish cooking. When done cooking, toss the broccoli beef with the mandarin oranges and green onions. Serve over white rice.

GRANDMOTHER'S STUFFED PEPPERS

COOK ON LOW
8 TO 10 HOURS

makes 5 servings

Fresh vegetables partner with beef and peppers in a delicious tomato sauce.

½ lb.	ground beef
1 medium	yellow onion, chopped
1 medium	carrot, diced
1 large	tomato, diced
1 cup	fresh or frozen corn kernels
1 cup	cooked white rice
1 cup	ketchup
2 cloves	garlic, minced
1 tsp.	salt
1 tsp.	freshly ground black pepper
1 Tbs.	fresh oregano, minced
2 Tbs.	fresh Italian parsley, minced
6 tall	green bell peppers, cored, seeds and pith removed
10¾ oz. can	condensed tomato soup

•••*To increase this recipe, double all ingredients except the soup and use the 5, 6 or 7-quart Crock-Pot® slow cooker. The peppers should fit comfortably upright in the stoneware.*

In a large mixing bowl, combine all the ingredients except the bell peppers and tomato soup. Stuff each bell pepper with the mixture and place the peppers standing upright side-by-side in the Crock-Pot® slow cooker. Pour the undiluted tomato soup over the peppers. Cover; cook on Low for 6 to 8 hours (or on High for 3 to 4 hours).

PORK LOIN WITH SHERRY & RED ONIONS

makes 8 servings

A simple sauce brings out the best of mild-flavored pork loin.

3 large	red onions, thinly sliced
1 cup	pearl onions, blanched and peeled
2 Tbs.	unsalted butter or margarine
½ tsp.	salt
½ tsp.	freshly ground black pepper
2½ lbs.	boneless pork loin, tied
½ cup	cooking sherry
2 Tbs.	Italian parsley, chopped
1½ Tbs.	cornstarch
2 Tbs.	water

•••*To increase this recipe, double all ingredients except the sherry, cornstarch and water. Use a 5, 6 or 7-quart Crock-Pot® slow cooker.*

In a medium skillet, sauté the red onions and pearl onions in the butter until soft. Season with salt and pepper. Rub the pork loin with salt and pepper to taste and place in the Crock-Pot® slow cooker. Add the sautéed onions, sherry and parsley. Cover; cook on Low 8 to 10 hours (or on High for 5 to 6 hours). Remove the pork loin from the stoneware and let stand 15 minutes before slicing. Combine the cornstarch and water and add to the juices in the stoneware to thicken the sauce. Cook on High for 10 minutes, stirring occasionally. Serve the pork loin with the onions and sherry sauce.

CARIBBEAN PORK CHOPS

makes 4 servings

COOK ON LOW
7 TO 9 HOURS

These chops get their spice from the inclusion of a Scotch Bonnet chile pepper, which is one of the hottest chile peppers available, often used in Caribbean cooking. If a Scotch Bonnet is unavailable, use a Habañero chile pepper. Use care while seeding and chopping the chile to avoid getting the fiery oil on your hands or in your eyes.

1 tsp.	ground allspice
1 tsp.	freshly ground black pepper
1 tsp.	ground cinnamon
½ tsp.	ground nutmeg
2 tsp.	dried thyme
½ cup	scallions, finely chopped
3 Tbs.	soy sauce
2 Tbs.	fresh ginger, grated
1	Scotch Bonnet (or Habañero) chile pepper, seeded and minced
2 Tbs.	garlic, minced
2 tsp.	sugar
1 tsp.	salt
4 lean	pork chops, 1-inch thick

•••*To increase this recipe, double all ingredients and use a
5, 6 or 7-quart Crock-Pot® slow cooker.*

In a food processor, combine all of the herbs and spices with the scallions, soy sauce, fresh ginger, chile pepper, garlic, sugar and salt, and process to a coarse paste. Coat the pork chops with the paste and place in the Crock-Pot® slow cooker. Cover; cook on Low 7 to 9 hours (or on High for 4 to 5 hours).

POLYNESIAN PORK ROAST

makes 8 servings

Pineapple and citrus flavors give this pork roast sweet and mellow undertones. Serve with white rice and a fresh green salad for a satisfying meal.

¼ cup	soy sauce
1 tsp.	liquid smoke
20 oz. can	crushed pineapple, drained
¼ cup	fresh orange juice
¼ cup	fresh lemon juice
1 Tbs.	orange zest, grated
1 Tbs.	lemon zest, grated
3 Tbs.	sugar
2 Tbs.	cornstarch
3 lbs.	boneless pork shoulder roast (Boston butt)

•••*To increase this recipe, double all the ingredients except the cornstarch.*
Increase the cornstarch to 3 tablespoons and proceed as directed.
Use the 6 or 7-quart Crock-Pot® slow cooker.

In a medium saucepan, combine the soy sauce, liquid smoke, pineapple, orange juice, lemon juice, orange zest, lemon zest, sugar and cornstarch. Whisk and bring the mixture to a boil, stirring constantly until thickened.

Place the pork roast in the Crock-Pot® slow cooker and pour half of the fruit glaze over the roast. Reserve the remaining glaze. Cover; cook on Low 8 to 10 hours (or on High for 4 to 5 hours). Warm the remaining glaze on low heat and serve over the pork.

Rosemary Mustard Pork Roast

Cook on Low
6 to 8 hours

makes 6 servings

Pork becomes tender and moist when cooked in the Crock-Pot® slow cooker. This recipe, with mustard, rosemary, garlic and tarragon, creates a medley of savory flavors.

3 medium	Yukon gold potatoes, quartered
3 medium	carrots, cut into 1-inch pieces
1 medium	yellow onion, cut into eighths
¼ cup	whole grain mustard
2 cloves	garlic, minced
2 tsp.	dried rosemary
½ tsp.	dried tarragon
1 tsp.	kosher salt
1 tsp.	freshly ground black pepper
2½ lbs.	boneless pork roast, trimmed of fat

•••*To increase this recipe, double all ingredients and use a 5, 6 or 7-quart Crock-Pot® slow cooker.*

Place the potatoes, carrots, and onion in the bottom of the Crock-Pot® slow cooker. In a small bowl, combine the mustard, garlic, rosemary, tarragon, salt, and pepper. Pat the pork roast dry and coat with the mustard mixture. Place on top of the vegetables. Cover; cook on Low 6 to 8 hours (or on High 3 to 4 hours).

COOK ON LOW
6 TO 8 HOURS

PINEAPPLE-CRANBERRY PORK CHOPS

makes 4 servings

Pineapple and cranberry sauce combine to form a tangy, sweet sauce for these tender pork chops.

4 boneless	center-cut pork chops, about ½-inch thick
½ tsp.	salt
½ tsp.	freshly ground black pepper
1 Tbs.	extra-virgin olive oil
10 oz. can	crushed pineapple
1 cup	canned whole cranberry sauce
1 medium	red onion, thinly sliced

Season the chops with the salt and pepper. In a large skillet, heat the olive oil on medium-high heat and brown the chops, about 2-3 minutes per side. Place the chops in the Crock-Pot® slow cooker. In a medium bowl, combine the remaining ingredients and pour over the chops. Cover; cook on Low 6 to 8 hours (or on High 3 to 4 hours).

HARVEST APPLES, ONIONS & PORK TENDERLOIN

makes 6 servings

The flavors of autumn shine through in this satisfying pork tenderloin dish.

2 lbs.	pork tenderloins
½ tsp.	kosher salt
½ tsp.	freshly ground black pepper
2 Tbs.	dark brown sugar
1 Tbs.	cider vinegar
½ cup	golden raisins
1 medium	Granny Smith apple, peeled, cored and chopped
1 medium	sweet potato, peeled and chopped
1 medium	red onion, chopped

•••*To increase this recipe, double all ingredients and use a
5, 6 or 7-quart Crock-Pot® slow cooker.*

Season the tenderloins with salt and pepper and place in the Crock-Pot® slow cooker. In a medium bowl, combine the remaining ingredients, mixing well. Spoon over the tenderloins. Cover; cook on Low 6 to 8 hours (or on High 3 to 4 hours). Remove the tenderloins to serving platter and slice on the bias against the grain of the meat. Spoon the sauce over the slices before serving.

COOK ON LOW
8 TO 10 HOURS

WHITE BEAN & HAM SOUP

makes 4 servings

Hearty and full of smoky flavor, this bean soup will please the entire family. Serve with crusty bread and a green salad to round out the meal.

½ lb.	cannellini or Great Northern beans, soaked overnight
1	ham shank or ham hock, cut into pieces
1 medium	carrot, diced
1 medium	yellow onion, diced
2 ribs	celery, diced
2 cloves	garlic, sliced
1 quart	water
1 tsp.	salt
1 tsp.	freshly ground black pepper
1 tsp.	Herbes de Provence

•••*To increase this recipe, double all ingredients and use a 5, 6 or 7-quart Crock-Pot® slow cooker.*

Place the beans, ham shank, carrot, onion, celery, garlic, and water in the Crock-Pot® slow cooker. Cover; Cook on Low 8 to 10 hours (or on High 4 to 5 hours). Season to taste with the salt, pepper, and Herbes de Provence before serving.

Lamb Shank Tangine

COOK ON LOW
8 TO 10 HOURS

makes 4 servings

The Crock-Pot® slow cooker functions as a Moroccan tagine in this indulgent dish. These succulent lamb shanks will fall apart at the bone and are bathed in a savory sweet broth. Serve with couscous and a fresh green salad.

4	lamb shanks
2 medium	carrots, cut into ½-inch slices
1 large	yellow onion, diced
4 Tbs.	fresh ginger, grated
6 cloves	garlic, roughly chopped
2 Tbs.	ground cumin
1 Tbs.	ground cinnamon
1 cup	black raisins
1 cup	black olives
3 cups	chicken broth
¼ cup	fresh lemon juice
1 Tbs.	sugar
1 tsp.	salt
1 tsp.	freshly ground pepper

•••To increase this recipe, double all ingredients except the chicken broth and lemon juice. Use a 5, 6 or 7-quart Crock-Pot® slow cooker.

In a large skillet over high heat, quickly brown the lamb shanks. Remove the lamb shanks. In the same skillet, sauté the carrots, onions, ginger and garlic. Add the spices to awaken their aroma. In the Crock-Pot® slow cooker, combine the lamb shanks, sautéed vegetable mixture, raisins, olives, chicken broth, lemon juice, sugar, salt and pepper. Cover; cook on Low 8 to 10 hours (or on High for 4 to 5 hours).

COOK ON HIGH
1 HOUR & LOW
10 TO 12 HOURS

STUFFED LAMB ROAST

makes 8 servings

The addition of lemon zest, rosemary and mint brighten the flavors of the stuffing for this lovely lamb roast.

3 lbs.	lamb roast, de-boned
1 medium	yellow onion, finely chopped
⅛ cup	unsalted butter or margarine, softened
½ cup	unseasoned soft bread crumbs
1	egg, beaten
1 tsp.	salt
1 tsp.	freshly ground black pepper
1 Tbs.	fresh rosemary, minced
1 Tbs.	fresh mint, minced
1 Tbs.	lemon zest, grated
1 Tbs.	extra-virgin olive oil
3 cloves	garlic, minced
2 ribs	celery, thinly sliced
1 medium	carrot, finely chopped
	salt and pepper to taste

•••*To increase this recipe, double all ingredients and use a
5, 6 or 7-quart Crock-Pot® slow cooker.*

Remove the excess fat from the lamb roast. In a medium mixing bowl, combine the remaining ingredients to form a stuffing. Stuff the lamb with the mixture, patting it into the roast securely. Roll the lamb and fasten with skewers or string and season with salt and pepper. Place the roast in the Crock-Pot® slow cooker and cook on High for 1 hour, then turn to Low for 10 to 12 hours. Let the lamb rest for 15 minutes before slicing. Pour the natural juices over the roast to serve.

LAMB CHOPS WITH RED WINE GLAZE

COOK ON LOW
6 TO 8 HOURS

makes 6 servings

When cooking with wine, select a high quality wine that would be equally enjoyable to drink.
A delicious Merlot wine splendidly accents the rich qualities of the lamb and mushrooms in this dish.

6	lamb rib chops
2 Tbs.	extra-virgin olive oil
2 cups	crimini mushrooms, sliced
	(or portobello mushrooms, if available)
½ cup	red wine, preferably Merlot
2 tsp.	salt
2 cloves	garlic, minced
1 Tbs.	honey
1 tsp.	dried marjoram
1 tsp.	dried oregano
1 tsp.	dried basil

•••*To increase this recipe, double all ingredients and use a*
5, 6 or 7-quart Crock-Pot® slow cooker.

In a large skillet, brown the lamb chops in the oil. Drain well and remove the chops. Sauté the mushrooms in the same skillet until most of the moisture has been released. In a small mixing bowl, whisk together the red wine, salt, garlic, honey, marjoram, oregano and basil. Place the chops and mushrooms in the Crock-Pot® slow cooker and cover with the wine glaze. Cover; cook on Low for 6 to 8 hours (or on High for 3 to 4 hours). Serve the lamb chops with the mushrooms and drizzle with the wine glaze.

COOK ON LOW
4 TO 6 HOURS

IRISH LAMB STEW

makes 6 servings

Serve with Irish soda bread or peasant bread to sop up the delicious juices.

6 large slices	bacon, diced
¼ cup	all-purpose flour
½ tsp.	salt
½ tsp.	freshly ground black pepper
2 lbs.	boneless lamb shoulder, cut into 1-inch cubes
1 cup	beef broth
1 cup	white wine
1½ cups	frozen pearl onions, thawed
3 medium	carrots, cut into 1-inch pieces
3 medium	potatoes, cut into 1-inch chunks
3 cloves	fresh garlic, sliced
2 whole	bay leaves
1 tsp.	dried thyme
½ tsp.	salt
½ tsp.	freshly ground black pepper

•••*To increase this recipe, double all ingredients and use a
5, 6 or 7-quart Crock-Pot® slow cooker.*

In a medium skillet, cook the diced bacon until the fat has rendered and the bacon is crispy. Remove the bacon and set aside. Combine the flour, salt and black pepper. Dredge the lamb cubes in the flour mixture and brown in the bacon fat in the same skillet. Remove the lamb from the skillet and set aside. Deglaze the skillet with the beef broth and white wine.

Place the lamb, bacon, and the beef broth mixture in the Crock-Pot® slow cooker and add the remaining ingredients. Mix thoroughly to combine. Cover; cook on Low 4 to 6 hours (or on High for 2 to 3 hours). Skim any excess fat off the top of the stew and remove the bay leaves before serving.

CHAPTER FOUR
Tempting Poultry Entrées

Chipotle & Lime Chicken Breasts

makes 4 servings

Cook on Low
6 to 8 hours

A sophisticated meal with a Latin-inspired list of ingredients.

1 lb. small	red skinned potatoes, quartered
4	boneless, skinless chicken breasts
1	chipotle pepper, finely minced
2 Tbs.	adobo sauce (from the can of chipotle peppers)
1 Tbs.	fresh lime juice
¼ cup	heavy cream
½ cup	sour cream
12 oz.	baby spinach leaves, cleaned

Place the potatoes and chicken breasts in the Crock-Pot® slow cooker. In a small bowl, combine the minced chipotle, adobo sauce, lime juice, and heavy cream. Pour over the chicken breasts. Cover; cook on Low 6 to 8 hours (or on High 3 to 4 hours). Remove the potatoes and chicken breasts and set aside, covering to keep warm.

Remove all but 1 cup of liquid in the stoneware and discard. To the reserved liquid, add the sour cream and baby spinach leaves, mixing well to combine. Turn to High and cook about 5 to 10 minutes, or until the spinach has wilted and the sauce is warm throughout. Pour the creamy spinach sauce over the chicken and potatoes and serve immediately.

COOK ON LOW
6 TO 8 HOURS

CHICKEN PAPRIKASH

makes 4 to 6 servings

A Hungarian chicken dish full of warm, exotic flavor with a hint of creaminess.
Serve with egg noodles or dumplings.

1 whole	fryer chicken, about 3 lbs., cut into 8 pieces
1 clove	garlic, crushed
2 large	yellow onions, thinly sliced
2 Tbs.	sweet Hungarian paprika
½ tsp.	salt
¼ cup	chicken broth
¼ cup	sour cream

In the Crock-Pot® slow cooker, combine the chicken, garlic, onions, paprika, salt, and chicken broth. Cover; cook on low 6 to 8 hours (or on High 3 to 4 hours). Remove the chicken and set aside, covering to keep warm. Skim off any fat from the liquid remaining. Add the sour cream to the remaining juices in the stoneware, whisking to combine. Turn to High and heat until the sauce is warmed throughout, about 10 minutes. Pour the sauce over the chicken before serving.

CLASSIC CHICKEN & DUMPLINGS

COOK ON LOW
6 TO 8 HOURS

makes 4 servings

A comfort food classic that's an easy slam-dunk in the Crock-Pot® slow cooker. Don't be surprised when your family asks for this meal over and over again.

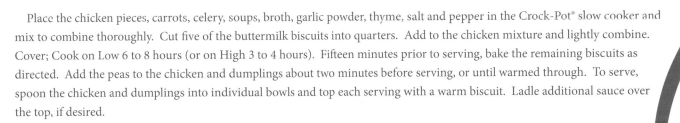

2	boneless, skinless chicken breasts, cut into bite-sized pieces
2 medium	carrots, cut into 1-inch slices
2 ribs	celery, sliced
10¾ oz. can	condensed cream of mushroom soup
10¾ oz. can	condensed cream of chicken soup
1½ cups	chicken broth
½ tsp.	garlic powder
½ tsp.	dried thyme
½ tsp.	kosher salt
½ tsp.	freshly ground black pepper
16 oz. can	refrigerated buttermilk biscuits
½ cup	frozen green peas

Place the chicken pieces, carrots, celery, soups, broth, garlic powder, thyme, salt and pepper in the Crock-Pot® slow cooker and mix to combine thoroughly. Cut five of the buttermilk biscuits into quarters. Add to the chicken mixture and lightly combine. Cover; Cook on Low 6 to 8 hours (or on High 3 to 4 hours). Fifteen minutes prior to serving, bake the remaining biscuits as directed. Add the peas to the chicken and dumplings about two minutes before serving, or until warmed through. To serve, spoon the chicken and dumplings into individual bowls and top each serving with a warm biscuit. Ladle additional sauce over the top, if desired.

COOK ON LOW
8 TO 10 HOURS

SAVORY CHICKEN CHILI

makes 8 servings

Also called "white chili," this combination of chicken, white beans, and Southwest seasonings is a nice twist on the traditional. Serve with cheese quesadillas.

3 15 oz. cans	Great Northern or cannellini beans, drained
2 cups	cooked chicken, chopped
1 medium	yellow onion, chopped
2 medium	red peppers, seeded and chopped
4 oz. can	diced green chilies
3 cloves	garlic, minced
3½ cups	chicken broth
2 tsp.	ground cumin
1 tsp.	salt
1 tsp.	dried oregano

•••*To increase this recipe, double all ingredients and use a 5, 6 or 7-quart Crock-Pot® slow cooker.*

Combine all ingredients in the Crock-Pot® slow cooker. Mix thoroughly. Cover; cook on Low 8 to 10 hours (or on High for 4 to 5 hours).

HERBED GARLIC CHICKEN

COOK ON LOW
8 TO 10 HOURS

makes 4 servings

This simple chicken entrée is infused with garlic and herbs.

⅛ cup	butter or margarine, softened
8 cloves	garlic, minced
1 Tbs.	fresh rosemary leaves, chopped
½ tsp.	salt
½ tsp.	freshly ground pepper
3 lbs.	whole chicken, cleaned
1 cup	chicken broth
3 Tbs.	fresh lemon juice
6 small	red potatoes, halved
2 Tbs.	chives, minced, for garnish

•••*To increase this recipe, double all ingredients except the lemon juice and use a 5, 6 or 7-quart Crock-Pot® slow cooker.*

In a small mixing bowl, combine the butter, garlic, rosemary, salt and pepper until well-incorporated. Rub the compound butter under and over the skin of the chicken and in the cavity. Place the chicken, chicken broth, lemon juice and potatoes in the Crock-Pot® slow cooker. Cover; heat on Low 8 to 10 hours (or on High for 3½ to 5 hours). Remove the chicken and potatoes with a large slotted spoon. Cut the chicken into pieces and garnish with the chives before serving.

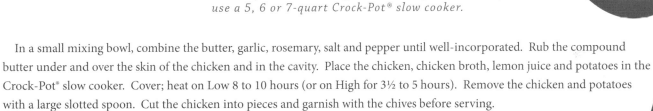

ROAST CHICKEN WITH PEAS, PROSCIUTTO AND CREAM

makes 6 servings

This sophisticated dish is surprisingly simple to make.
The rustic taste of the prosciutto beautifully balances the creaminess of the chicken.

2 Tbs.	unsalted butter or margarine, melted
2½ lbs.	whole chicken, cleaned and seasoned with salt and pepper
1 small	yellow onion, finely chopped
5 oz.	prosciutto or bacon, diced
½ cup	dry white wine
10 oz. pkg.	frozen peas
½ cup	heavy cream
1½ Tbs.	cornstarch
2 Tbs.	water
4 cups	farfalle (bowtie) pasta or pasta of your choice, cooked al denté

•••To increase this recipe, double all ingredients except the white wine and cream, and use a 5, 6 or 7-quart Crock-Pot® slow cooker.

In a large skillet, melt the butter and add the whole chicken. Turn and brown the chicken over medium heat. Remove and place the chicken in the Crock-Pot® slow cooker. Add the onion, prosciutto or bacon and wine. Cover; cook on Low 8 to 10 hours (or on High for 3½ to 4 hours).

In the last 30 minutes of cooking, add the frozen peas and heavy cream to the liquid in the stoneware. Stir, cover and continue cooking. When done, remove the chicken from the stoneware and carve the meat in slices. Combine the cornstarch and water and add to the juice in the stoneware to thicken the sauce. Heat on High for 10 minutes, stirring occasionally. To serve, spoon the pasta onto individual plates, place the chicken over the pasta and top each portion with sauce.

GREEN TOMATILLO CHICKEN

makes 6 servings

COOK ON LOW
6 TO 8 HOURS

This exceptional dish pairs chicken with a creamy tomatillo sauce. Serve with Spanish rice and earthy, roasted vegetables for a beautiful meal.

6	boneless, skinless chicken breasts
1 medium	yellow onion, sliced
2 cloves	garlic, minced
1 tsp.	ground cumin
1 tsp.	dried oregano
1 tsp.	salt
1 tsp.	freshly ground pepper
1 Tbs.	fresh lemon juice
1 cup	green tomatillo salsa
1½ cups	sour cream

•••*To increase this recipe, double all ingredients and use a
5, 6 or 7-quart Crock-Pot® slow cooker.*

Place the chicken breasts in the Crock-Pot® slow cooker. In a small mixing bowl, combine the onion, garlic, cumin, oregano, salt, pepper, lemon juice and salsa. Pour the sauce over the chicken breasts. Cook on Low 6 to 8 hours (or on High for 3 to 4 hours). Remove the chicken from the stoneware and keep warm. Stir the sour cream into the juices in the stoneware and blend well. Cook on High for 8 minutes, stirring frequently. Pour the sauce over the chicken and serve immediately.

COOK ON LOW
4 TO 6 HOURS

COQ AU VIN

makes 6 servings

Literally meaning, "chicken in wine," this country French classic is heaven in a bowl.

½ lb.	bacon, diced
¼ cup	all-purpose flour
½ tsp.	salt
½ tsp.	freshly ground black pepper
2 lbs.	fryer chicken, cut into pieces
1 cup	dry red wine
½ cup	chicken broth
2 Tbs.	tomato paste
1½ cups	frozen peeled pearl onions
3 medium	carrots, cut into 1-inch pieces
8 large	white mushrooms, sliced in half
½ tsp.	dried thyme
½ tsp.	dried oregano
¼ cup	fresh parsley, minced

•••*To increase this recipe, double all ingredients and use a
5, 6 or 7-quart Crock-Pot® slow cooker.*

In a medium skillet, cook the diced bacon until the fat has rendered and the bacon is crispy. Remove the bacon and set aside. Combine the flour, salt and black pepper. Dredge the chicken pieces in the flour mixture and brown in the bacon fat in the same skillet. Remove the chicken and bacon and set aside. Deglaze the skillet with the red wine and chicken broth, bringing the liquids up to a boil and scraping the bottom of the skillet. Whisk in the tomato paste.

Place the chicken, bacon, onions, carrots, mushrooms, thyme, and oregano in the Crock-Pot® slow cooker. Pour the sauce over the chicken and vegetables, stirring to combine. Cover; cook on Low 4 to 6 hours (or on High for 2 to 3 hours). Before serving, skim off any excess fat on the surface. Add the fresh parsley before serving.

APPLE CHICKEN CURRY

COOK ON LOW
6 TO 8 HOURS

makes 4 servings

A delicate blend of sweetness and spice and sure to please any mealtime guest.
Serve with basmati rice and Indian flatbread.

1 medium	yellow onion, sliced
1 Tbs.	extra-virgin olive oil
1 Tbs.	curry powder, divided
4	skinless, boneless, chicken breast halves
½ tsp.	kosher salt
½ tsp.	freshly ground black pepper
½ lb.	small red potatoes, quartered
1 large	tart cooking apple, chopped
⅓ cup	golden raisins
1 cup	sour cream
2 Tbs.	fresh cilantro, minced

•••*To increase this recipe, double all ingredients and use a*
5, 6 or 7-quart Crock-Pot® slow cooker.

In a small skillet, sauté the sliced onion in the olive oil on medium heat, about 7 minutes. Season with 1 teaspoon of the curry powder. Season the chicken with the remaining curry powder, salt, and pepper. Place the potatoes, apple and raisins in the Crock-Pot® slow cooker, and add the seasoned chicken and onions. Cover; cook on Low for 6 to 8 hours (or on High 3 to 4 hours).

Prior to serving, remove the chicken and potatoes and set aside, covering to keep warm. Add the sour cream to the remaining juices in the stoneware, whisking until smooth. Cook on High for 10 minutes or until warmed throughout. To serve, spoon the sour cream sauce over the chicken and potatoes and garnish with the cilantro.

HONEY HOISIN CHICKEN

makes 6 servings

This Asian chicken dish goes well with bok choy, broccoli or asparagus on the side.

6 whole	boneless, skinless chicken breasts
3 Tbs.	soy sauce
3 Tbs.	honey
3 Tbs.	hoisin sauce
2 Tbs.	dry white wine
1 Tbs.	fresh ginger, grated
1 tsp.	freshly ground black pepper
6 cups	prepared, hot white rice
2 Tbs.	sesame seeds, toasted

•••*To increase this recipe, double all ingredients and use a
5, 6 or 7-quart Crock-Pot® slow cooker.*

Combine all ingredients in the Crock-Pot® slow cooker. Cover; cook on Low 4 to 6 hours (or on High for 2 to 3 hours). Halfway through cooking, turn the chicken breasts in the sauce to thoroughly re-coat. Once cooked, remove the chicken from the sauce and carve the chicken into slices. Serve over fluffy, hot white rice. Sprinkle with the toasted sesame seeds.

APRICOT MUSTARD CHICKEN

COOK ON LOW
7 TO 9 HOURS

makes 6 servings

Piquant spices are tempered by sweet apricot juice... a perfect combination to highlight the chicken breasts.

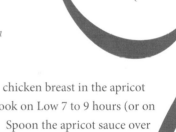

11½ oz. can	apricot juice/nectar
2 Tbs.	Dijon mustard
1 clove	garlic, minced
¼ tsp.	fresh ginger, grated
¼ tsp.	cayenne pepper
⅛ tsp.	ground allspice
⅛ tsp.	ground turmeric
⅛ tsp.	ground cardamom
6	boneless, skinless chicken breasts
4 cups	prepared couscous or wild rice blend

*•••To increase this recipe, double all ingredients and use a
5, 6 or 7-quart Crock-Pot® slow cooker.*

In a mixing bowl, whisk together the apricot nectar, mustard, garlic, ginger and spices. Dip each chicken breast in the apricot mixture and place in Crock-Pot® slow cooker. Pour the remaining sauce over the breasts. Cover; cook on Low 7 to 9 hours (or on High for 4 to 5 hours). Remove the chicken from the stoneware and arrange over rice or couscous. Spoon the apricot sauce over the chicken breasts before serving.

CHICKEN PROVENÇAL

makes 8 servings

From southern France, this chicken entrée contrasts the citrus with the sweet. Serve with a crusty French baguette and seasonal vegetables.

2 lbs.	skinless, boneless chicken thighs, each cut into quarters
2 medium	red peppers, cut into ¼-inch thick slices
1 medium	yellow pepper, cut into ¼-inch thick slices
1	yellow onion, thinly sliced
28 oz. can	plum tomatoes, drained
3 cloves	garlic, minced
¼ tsp.	salt
¼ tsp.	dried thyme
¼ tsp.	fennel seeds, crushed
3 strips	orange peel
½ cup	fresh basil leaves, chopped

•••*To increase this recipe, double all ingredients and use a
5, 6 or 7-quart Crock-Pot® slow cooker.*

Place all the ingredients in the Crock-Pot® slow cooker, except for the basil leaves. Mix thoroughly. Cover; cook on Low 7 to 9 hours (or on High for 3 to 4 hours). Before serving, garnish with the fresh basil leaves.

Chicken Cordon Bleu Rolls

makes 6 servings

COOK ON LOW
4 TO 6 HOURS

These delicious rolls are easy to make, yet will impress the most discerning guests. Serve with wild rice and asparagus for an elegant meal.

6	chicken breasts, pounded to ¼-inch thickness
6 slices	prosciutto
6 thin slices	Swiss cheese
	salt and pepper to taste
½ can (10¾ oz.)	condensed cream of mushroom soup
¼ cup	milk
¼ cup	dry white wine

•••To increase this recipe, double the chicken breasts, prosciutto and Swiss cheese and use the 5, 6 or 7-quart Crock-Pot® Slow Cooker. Do not increase any of the remaining ingredients.

Place one chicken breast on a piece of waxed paper. Place one slice of prosciutto on the chicken and cover with one slice of cheese. Roll up the stuffed chicken breast and secure with a wooden pick or cooking string. Repeat with the remaining chicken breasts. Season each roll with salt and pepper. Arrange the rolls in the Crock-Pot® slow cooker. In a small bowl, whisk together the soup, milk and white wine. Pour the sauce over the chicken breast rolls. Cover; cook on Low 4 to 6 hours (or on High for 3 to 4 hours).

COOK ON LOW
4 TO 6 HOURS

MANGO GINGER CHICKEN

makes 4 servings

Tropical flavors are the star of this chicken dish. Serve with rice or noodles to soak up the delicious mango sauce.

1½ cups	frozen mango slices
4	boneless, skinless chicken breasts
2 Tbs.	soy sauce
1 Tbs.	dark brown sugar
1 Tbs.	fresh ginger, grated
1 clove	garlic, minced
2	green onions, thinly sliced, for garnish

Place the mango slices in bottom of the Crock-Pot® slow cooker. Place the chicken breasts on top of the slices. In a small bowl, combine the remaining ingredients except the green onions, and pour over the chicken. Cover; cook on Low 4 to 6 hours (or on High 2 to 3 hours). To serve, place the chicken breasts on a serving platter and spoon the mango sauce over the top. Garnish with the green onions before serving.

CHEESY CHICKEN & VEGETABLES

makes 4 servings

COOK ON LOW
6 TO 8 HOURS

A cheese-sauced entrée laced with colorful veggies.

4	boneless, skinless chicken breasts
1 tsp.	salt
½ tsp.	freshly ground black pepper
½ tsp.	garlic powder
16 oz. pkg.	frozen mixed vegetables
10¾ oz. can	cream of chicken soup
10¾ oz. can	cheddar cheese soup
½ cup	dry white wine

•••*To increase this recipe, double all ingredients and use the 5, 6 or 7 quart Crock-Pot® slow cooker.*

Season the chicken breasts with the salt, pepper and garlic powder. Place the vegetables, soups and wine in the Crock-Pot® slow cooker. Stir well to combine and add the chicken breasts, spooning the vegetables and sauce over the chicken. Cover; cook on Low 6 to 8 hours (or on High for 3 to 4 hours).

PESTO-STUFFED CHICKEN BREASTS

COOK ON LOW
4 TO 6 HOURS

makes 6 servings

Classic Italian flavors – cheese, pesto, wine and pine nuts – highlight this easy entrée.

1 cup	ricotta cheese
¼ cup	Parmesan cheese, grated
½ cup	prepared pesto sauce
6	chicken breasts, pounded thin
	salt and pepper
½ can (10¾ oz.)	condensed cream of mushroom soup
¼ cup	milk
¼ cup	white wine
	toasted pine nuts, for garnish
	fresh basil leaves, for garnish

•••*To increase this recipe, double the chicken breasts, ricotta, Parmesan and pesto and use a 5, 6 or 7-quart Crock-Pot® slow cooker. Do not increase any other ingredients.*

In a small mixing bowl, combine the ricotta, Parmesan cheese and pesto. Place a dollop of the pesto-ricotta mixture on each chicken breast. Roll up each chicken breast and secure with a wooden pick or cooking string. Season each roll with salt and pepper. Arrange the rolls in the Crock-Pot® slow cooker. In a small bowl, whisk together the soup, milk and white wine. Pour the sauce over the chicken breast rolls. Cover; cook on Low 4 to 6 hours (or on High for 3 to 4 hours). Garnish each chicken breast with toasted pine nuts and fresh basil leaves.

CHICKEN & VEGETABLE LASAGNA

makes 8 to 10 servings

A creamy white sauce, chicken and fresh vegetables present a sly twist to traditional lasagna.

1 large	yellow onion, chopped
1 medium	zucchini, diced
1 medium	carrot, diced
2 cloves	garlic, minced
2½ cups	cooked chicken, shredded
1 Tbs.	fresh oregano, minced
2 Tbs.	fresh Italian parsley, minced
1 Tbs.	fresh thyme, minced
1 tsp.	salt
1 tsp.	freshly ground black pepper
10 oz. pkg.	lasagna noodles, cooked al denté, drained and cut into thirds
	cooking spray

White Sauce:

2 Tbs.	butter or margarine, melted
2 Tbs.	all-purpose flour
1 tsp.	salt
1 cup	milk
2 cups	shredded mozzarella cheese, divided
12 oz. carton	cottage cheese

•••*To increase this recipe, double all ingredients except the sauce. Increase the sauce ingredients by half. Use a 5, 6 or 7-quart Crock-Pot® slow cooker.*

In a medium skillet, sauté the onion, zucchini, carrot and garlic until tender. Add the chicken and season with the oregano, parsley, thyme, salt and pepper. Coat the Crock-Pot® slow cooker with cooking spray. Cover the bottom of the stoneware with lasagna noodles and spoon one-third of the chicken and vegetables over the noodles. Repeat with the remaining noodles and chicken mixture.

In a medium mixing bowl, combine the butter, flour, salt, milk, 1 cup of the mozzarella cheese and the cottage cheese to make the white sauce. Pour the sauce over the chicken and vegetables in the stoneware. Do not stir. Cover; cook on Low 4 to 6 hours (or on High for 2 to 3 hours). During the last 30 minutes of cooking, top the lasagna with the remaining mozzarella cheese and turn to High. If desired, spoon into individual casseroles and broil the cheese just prior to serving.

Marinated Chinese Chicken Salad

makes 6 to 8 servings

Cool, crunchy lettuce and noodles are paired with savory chicken, then dressed with a tangy Asian-style vinaigrette. For faster prep time, substitute bottled Asian dressing.

Marinade:

3 cloves	garlic, minced
1 Tbs.	fresh ginger, grated
1 tsp.	dried red chile flakes
2 Tbs.	honey
3 Tbs.	soy sauce
2 Tbs.	sesame oil
6	boneless, skinless chicken breasts

Dressing:

⅓ cup	rice wine vinegar
1 clove	garlic, minced
1 tsp.	ginger, grated
1 Tbs.	honey

Salad:

1 large head	iceberg lettuce, shredded
2 medium	carrots, julienned
½ cup	roasted whole peanuts, chopped
¼ cup	fresh cilantro, chopped
½ pkg.	maifun noodles, fried in hot oil
	(substitute 6 oz. crispy Chinese noodles)

•••To increase this recipe, double all ingredients and use a 5, 6 or 7-quart Crock-Pot® slow cooker.

In a small mixing bowl, combine the marinade ingredients. Place the chicken in the Crock-Pot® slow cooker and pour the marinade over the chicken, coating each piece well. Cover; cook on Low 6 to 8 hours (or on High 3 to 4 hours). Remove the chicken from the stoneware and cool. Shred the chicken into bite-sized pieces and refrigerate until you assemble the salad.

In a small mixing bowl, combine the dressing ingredients with ½ cup of the juices from the stoneware. In a large serving bowl, toss together the shredded chicken, lettuce, carrots, peanuts, cilantro and maifun noodles. Shortly before serving, drizzle with the salad dressing. Toss well and serve.

COOK ON LOW
6 TO 8 HOURS

SIMPLE HERB-ROASTED CHICKEN

makes 4 servings

This is your go-to recipe for pre-cooked chicken. An excellent, economical alternative to buying cooked rotisserie chicken, you can slow cook the chicken and refrigerate or freeze until needed.

3-3½ lbs.	broiler/fryer chicken, cleaned and patted dry
1 tsp.	kosher salt
½ tsp.	freshly ground black pepper
1 tsp.	your favorite dried herbs, such as rosemary, thyme, oregano, etc.
1 head	garlic, cut in half
2	lemons, cut into quarters

···*To increase this recipe, double all ingredients and use a
5, 6 or 7-quart Crock-Pot® slow cooker.*

Season the inner and outer surfaces of the chicken with the salt, pepper, and herbs. Place the garlic halves and lemon quarters into the cavity of the chicken. Place the chicken, breast side up, in the Crock-Pot® slow cooker. Cover; Cook on Low 6 to 8 hours.

Remove the chicken. At this point, you can discard the skin and remove the meat from the bones before refrigerating or freezing. Or, you can serve the chicken in pieces. The remaining juices and drippings can be used for flavoring after the fat has been skimmed off. Tightly cover the juices and refrigerate or freeze until use.

BBQ Turkey Smokey Joes

makes 10 servings

Cook on Low
8 to 10 hours

Super open-faced sandwiches for the big game! Score a touchdown by serving with coleslaw and plenty of fries.

3 lbs.	ground turkey
1	yellow onion, finely chopped
1	green pepper, seeded and finely chopped
2 8 oz. cans	tomato sauce
¾ cup	ketchup
¼ cup	dark brown sugar, packed
3 Tbs.	cider vinegar
1 Tbs.	liquid smoke
1 Tbs.	Worcestershire sauce
1 tsp.	cayenne pepper
¼ tsp.	freshly ground black pepper
¼ tsp.	garlic powder
10	onion sandwich rolls, split and toasted

•••*Increase this recipe by doubling the turkey, onion, green pepper and seasonings.*
Use the 5, 6 or 7-quart Crock-Pot® slow cooker.

Brown the turkey in a skillet and drain off any remaining fat. Place the turkey in the Crock-Pot® slow cooker and add the remaining ingredients except the sandwich rolls. Stir thoroughly. Cover; cook on Low 8 to 10 hours (or on High for 3 to 4 hours). To serve, spoon the turkey and sauce over the rolls.

COOK ON LOW
6 TO 8 HOURS

TARRAGON-RUBBED TURKEY BREAST

makes 6 servings

Tarragon complements turkey beautifully in this simple presentation.
Serve with mashed potatoes to absorb the wonderful gravy.

½ tsp.	salt
½ tsp.	freshly ground black pepper
2 tsp.	dried tarragon
2 Tbs.	unsalted butter, softened
3-4 lbs.	boneless turkey breast
1 Tbs.	instant flour or 2 tsp. cornstarch
2 Tbs.	cold water
1 tsp.	gravy seasoning, such as Kitchen Bouquet™
	salt and pepper to taste

•••*To increase this recipe, double all ingredients and use a*
6 or 7-quart Crock-Pot® slow cooker.

In a small bowl, combine the salt, pepper, tarragon, and butter, until well-mixed. Rub the compound butter all over the turkey breast. Place the turkey in the Crock-Pot® slow cooker. Cover; cook on Low for 6 to 8 hours (or on High for 3 to 4 hours). Remove the turkey, cover with foil and keep warm.

Discard all but 1 cup of juices from the stoneware and turn to High. In a small bowl, whisk together the flour and cold water until smooth, and slowly whisk into the turkey juices. Heat until the sauce is smooth and thickened. Season with the gravy seasoning and add salt and pepper to taste. To serve, slice the turkey and spoon the sauce over the slices.

Turkey Madeira Tetrazzini

makes 8 servings

COOK ON LOW
6 TO 8 HOURS

Turkey is lean poultry with a very mild flavor so it pairs perfectly with a rich Madeira wine and cream sauce.

2 lbs.	turkey breast tenders
½ cup	chicken broth
¼ cup	Madeira wine
2 oz.	dried porcini mushrooms
1 medium	white onion, thinly sliced
½ cup	heavy cream
1 cup	fresh asparagus, cut in 2-inch pieces, cooked until tender-crisp
¼ cup	fresh Italian parsley, finely chopped
16 oz.	spaghetti noodles, cooked al denté and drained

···*To increase this recipe, double all ingredients and use a
5, 6 or 7-quart Crock-Pot® slow cooker.*

Place the turkey in the Crock-Pot® slow cooker. In a medium bowl, combine the chicken broth, wine, mushrooms, and onion. Pour the sauce over the turkey. Cover; cook on low 6 to 8 hours (or on High for 3 to 4 hours). Remove the turkey from the stoneware and cut into bite-sized pieces. Add the heavy cream, asparagus and parsley to the stoneware juices and mix thoroughly to combine. Return the turkey to the sauce. Cook on High until the sauce is warmed throughout. To serve, place the spaghetti noodles on a large serving platter and spoon the turkey and sauce over the pasta.

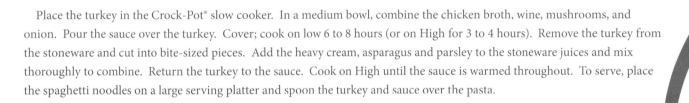

COOK ON HIGH
1 HOUR &
LOW 3 HOURS

TURKEY TAMALE PIE

makes 6 servings

An old family favorite, this dish uncovers flavors that are deep and satisfying.
For a more zesty flavor, add cayenne pepper to taste.

1 medium	yellow onion, chopped
1 clove	garlic, minced
1 Tbs.	vegetable oil
1 lb.	ground turkey
1 tsp.	freshly ground black pepper
¼ tsp.	cayenne pepper
¼ tsp.	salt
1 cup	yellow cornmeal
1½ cups	chicken broth
1	egg, beaten
14 oz. can	creamed corn
14 oz. can	plum tomatoes, drained and chopped
14 oz. can	black olives, drained

•••*To increase this recipe, double all ingredients and use a*
5, 6 or 7-quart Crock-Pot® slow cooker.

In a medium skillet, sauté the onion and garlic in the oil. Add the ground turkey and stir as the turkey browns. Season with the black pepper, cayenne pepper and salt. Drain any liquid from the skillet. In the Crock-Pot® slow cooker, combine the turkey mixture, cornmeal, broth, egg, creamed corn, plum tomatoes, and olives. Mix thoroughly. Cover; cook on High for 1 hour, then on Low for 3 hours.

LEMON-GARLIC TURKEY BREAST

COOK ON LOW
8 TO 10 HOURS

makes 6 servings

Pair this classic turkey with Thyme & Basil Herbed Rice (P.37).

3 lbs.	turkey breast
½ cup	lemon juice
6 cloves	garlic, minced
¼ tsp.	dried parsley
¼ tsp.	dried tarragon
¼ tsp.	dried rosemary
¼ tsp.	dried sage
¼ tsp.	salt
¼ tsp.	freshly ground black pepper
½ cup	white wine

•••*To increase this recipe, double all ingredients and use a
6 or 7-quart Crock-Pot® slow cooker.*

Place the turkey breast in the Crock-Pot® slow cooker. In a small bowl, combine the lemon juice, garlic, parsley, tarragon, rosemary, sage, salt, pepper and wine. Pour the sauce over the turkey breast. Cover; cook on Low 8 to 10 hours (or on High for 4 to 5 hours). Slice before serving.

CHAPTER FIVE

Flavorful Fish & Shellfish Entrées

VALENCIAN SEAFOOD PAELLA

COOK ON HIGH
2 TO 3 HOURS

makes 4 servings

Spanish paella is spectacular in this easy recipe with the addition of fresh seafood and small, but mighty ground saffron.

1 cup	long grain white rice
2 cups	water (you may substitute chicken broth, if desired)
1 small	yellow onion, diced
1 medium	tomato, diced
pinch	ground saffron
3 cloves	garlic, finely minced
¼ tsp.	cayenne pepper
1 tsp.	salt
1 tsp.	freshly ground black pepper
½ lb.	fresh mild fish fillets, cut into 1-inch pieces
½ lb.	fresh sea scallops, cleaned
½ lbs.	fresh mussels, scrubbed
½ lb.	fresh medium shrimp (uncooked), shelled and tails removed
8 oz.	frozen peas, thawed and drained
1	orange, cut in wedges

•••To increase this recipe, double all ingredients and use a 5, 6 or 7-quart Crock-Pot® slow cooker.

Place the rice, water, onion, tomato, saffron, garlic, cayenne pepper, salt and pepper in the Crock-Pot® slow cooker and mix thoroughly. Cook on High for 2 to 3 hours. Add the fish fillets, sea scallops, mussels, shrimp and peas to the paella and cook on High for 1 hour. Serve with orange wedges as a garnish.

SAN FRANCISCO CIOPPINO

makes 6 servings

Serve this California classic seafood stew with sourdough bread to mop up all the spicy juices.

28 oz. can	crushed tomatoes, undrained
8 oz. can	tomato sauce
1 medium	yellow onion, chopped
1 cup	white wine
1 cup	water
¼ cup	extra-virgin olive oil
½ cup	fresh Italian parsley, chopped
4 cloves	garlic, minced
2 tsp.	dried sweet basil
1 tsp.	dried thyme
1 tsp.	dried oregano
½ tsp.	red pepper flakes
½ tsp.	cayenne pepper
½ lb.	fresh or frozen cod or other whitefish fillets, thawed and cut into bite-sized pieces
⅓ lb.	fresh prawns, peeled and deveined
⅓ lb.	fresh sea scallops
½ lb.	fresh mussels, scrubbed
½ lb.	fresh clams, scrubbed
2	lemons, cut into wedges

*•••To increase this recipe, double all ingredients and use a
5, 6 or 7-quart Crock-Pot® slow cooker.*

Combine all ingredients, except the seafood and lemons, in the Crock-Pot® slow cooker. Cover; cook on Low 6 to 8 hours (or on High for 3 to 4 hours). Thirty minutes before serving, add the seafood to the stoneware and turn to High. To serve, squeeze lemon wedges into each serving.

Ginger-Soy Salmon Packets

Cook on Low
2 to 3 hours

makes 4 servings

These tasty packets open to reveal a robustly flavored salmon entrée inside, served perfectly with Asian accompaniments. Make extra to use in an Asian salad the next day.

2 Tbs.	soy sauce
1 Tbs.	sake or dry white wine
1 Tbs.	fresh ginger, grated
1 tsp.	toasted sesame oil
1 tsp.	toasted sesame seeds
1 clove	garlic, minced
4 6 oz.	salmon fillets
	sliced green onions for garnish
	heavy duty aluminum foil
	cooking spray

In a small bowl, combine the soy sauce, sake, ginger, sesame oil, sesame seeds, and garlic. Set aside.

Coat four 18 inch by 12 inch rectangles of heavy duty aluminum foil with cooking spray. Place each salmon fillet in the center of each aluminum foil rectangle. Lift the edges of the foil to make a bowl around the fillet and pour one-fourth of the soy sauce mixture over each salmon fillet. Seal the edges of the foil packet, making a tight ½-inch fold.

Place the foil packets in the Crock-Pot® slow cooker. Cover; cook on Low 2 to 3 hours (or on High for 1 hour). Carefully remove the foil packets with tongs – they will be hot. Place the each foil packet on a dinner plate and carefully open, avoiding the steam. Top each serving with sliced green onions.

COOK ON LOW
8 TO 10 HOURS

SHRIMP JAMBALAYA

makes 6 servings

A delicious combination of meat and shrimp, with a kick of spice. You can add more Tabasco® Sauce and cayenne pepper to reach your optimum level of spiciness.

12 oz.	boneless, skinless chicken breasts, cut into bite-sized pieces
8 oz.	smoked sausage of your choice
8 oz.	smoked ham, diced
1	green pepper, finely chopped
1 medium	yellow onion, chopped
2 ribs	celery, finely sliced
4 cloves	garlic, minced
14½ oz. can	whole tomatoes, undrained
⅓ cup	tomato paste
1 cup	chicken broth
1 Tbs.	dried parsley
1½ tsp.	dried basil leaves
½ tsp.	dried oregano leaves
1½ tsp.	Tabasco® Sauce
1½ tsp.	cayenne pepper
1 tsp.	black pepper
	salt to taste
1 lb.	fresh shrimp, shelled and cleaned
4 cups	cooked white or brown rice

*•••To increase this recipe, double all ingredients and use a
5, 6 or 7-quart Crock-Pot® slow cooker.*

Place the chicken and all remaining ingredients, except the shrimp and rice, in the Crock-Pot® slow cooker. Mix well to combine. Cover; cook on Low 8 to 10 hours (or on High for 3 to 4 hours). Add the shrimp during the last 30 minutes of cooking. Spoon the Shrimp Jambalaya over the rice when ready to serve.

Salmon Fettucine

makes 4 servings

Cook on Low
2 to 3 hours

Prep time is kept to a minimum while the compliments received will be at a maximum!

3 4 oz. cans	salmon, bones removed and flaked
10¾ oz. can	condensed cream of mushroom soup
1 cup	milk
1 tsp.	Dijon mustard
½ tsp.	kosher salt
½ tsp.	freshly ground black pepper
1 Tbs.	fresh dill, chopped
½ cup	frozen peas
½ cup	Parmesan cheese, freshly grated
1 lb.	fettucine pasta, cooked al dente and drained

Combine the salmon, soup, milk, mustard, salt, and pepper in the Crock-Pot® slow cooker until well-mixed. Cover; cook on Low 2 to 3 hours (or on High 1 hour). Five minutes before serving, add the dill, peas, and Parmesan cheese, mixing lightly. Serve over the hot pasta.

COOK ON LOW
6 TO 9 HOURS

CREAMY NEW ENGLAND CLAM CHOWDER

makes 4 servings

*This simple soup is hard to resist! The classic combination of clams, bacon and potatoes in a creamy soup
will leave a warm impression on your family and guests.*

3 slices	bacon, diced
1 medium	yellow onion, chopped
2 8 oz. cans	clams, drained
3 cloves	garlic, minced
3 medium	russet potatoes, pared and cubed
3 cups	water
1 tsp.	salt
½ tsp.	ground black pepper
13 oz. can	evaporated milk

•••*To increase this recipe, double all ingredients and use a
5, 6 or 7-quart Crock-Pot® slow cooker.*

In a small skillet, sauté the bacon and onion until golden. Drain and place in the Crock-Pot® slow cooker. Add all the remaining ingredients, except the evaporated milk. Stir well until combined. Cover; cook on Low 6 to 9 hours (or on High for 2 to 4 hours) or until the potatoes are tender. Add the evaporated milk during the last hour of cooking, stirring to blend. Cover and continue cooking until done.

Salmon & Parmesan Rice

makes 6 servings

Cook on High
1 Hour & Low
8 to 10 Hours

Perfect for a potluck or group gathering of any kind. Mix in the fresh tomatoes and green onions just before serving to add texture and color.

2 cups	long-grain converted white rice, uncooked
1 cup	cauliflower florets
1 cup	Parmesan cheese, grated
1 cup	dry white wine
1 cup	milk
1 cup	water
1 Tbs.	fresh tarragon, minced
1 tsp.	Dijon mustard
1½ tsp.	salt
½ tsp.	freshly ground black pepper
1 lb.	salmon fillet, cut into bite-sized pieces
1 cup	fresh tomatoes, diced
½ cup	green onions, thinly sliced

•••*To increase this recipe, double all ingredients and use a 5, 6 or 7-quart Crock-Pot® slow cooker.*

Combine all ingredients, except for the salmon, tomatoes and green onions, in the Crock-Pot® slow cooker. Mix thoroughly to blend. Cover; cook on High for 1 hour, then on Low for 6 to 8 hours (or on High for 3 to 4 hours). Thirty minutes prior to serving, add the salmon pieces. Cover and continue cooking. Before serving, stir in the tomatoes and green onions.

ASIAN SWEET & SOUR SHRIMP

makes 6 servings

Serve over jasmine, white or brown rice for a complete meal.

13 oz. can	pineapple, drained (reserve ½ cup of the juice)
2 ribs	celery, sliced
2 medium	tomatoes, cut into small wedges
1 cup	broccoli florets
1 medium	yellow onion, chopped
1 cup	chicken broth
3 cloves	garlic, minced
3 Tbs.	sugar
1 Tbs.	white vinegar
2 tsp.	fish sauce (optional)
2 tsp.	soy sauce
½ tsp.	fresh ginger, minced
½ lb.	medium shrimp, peeled and deveined
2 Tbs.	cornstarch
⅓ cup	water

•••*To increase this recipe, double all ingredients except the chicken broth and use a
5, 6 or 7-quart Crock-Pot® slow cooker.*

Combine all ingredients in Crock-Pot® slow cooker, except for the shrimp, cornstarch and water. Cover; cook on Low 4 to 6 hours (or on High for 2 to 3 hours). During the final 30 minutes of cooking, add the shrimp to the stoneware. Set the Crock-Pot® slow cooker to High. Whisk together the cornstarch and water and add to the sauce in the stoneware. Stir to blend until the sauce is thickened and hot throughout.

Halibut Steaks in a Lemony Wine Sauce

COOK ON HIGH
2½ TO 3 HOURS

makes 6 servings

Halibut is a firm white fish that deserves the bright flavors of lemon and wine.
Serve with seasonal vegetables and pasta or rice.

2 lbs.	fresh halibut steaks (or frozen, thawed steaks)
¼ cup	butter
2 Tbs.	flour
⅓ cup	dry white wine
⅓ cup	heavy cream
½ tsp.	salt
½ tsp.	freshly ground black pepper
¼ cup	fresh lemon juice
1 tsp.	lemon zest, grated
1 Tbs.	fresh sage, minced
1 Tbs.	fresh Italian parsley, minced

•••*To increase this recipe, double all ingredients and use a*
5, 6 or 7-quart Crock-Pot® slow cooker.

Pat halibut steaks dry and place in the Crock-Pot® slow cooker. In a medium saucepan, melt the butter and slowly whisk in the flour to create a roux. When slightly browned, add the wine and cream, constantly whisking over medium heat until the sauce has thickened. Add the salt, pepper, lemon juice, and lemon zest. Pour the sauce over the fish. Cover; cook on High 2½ to 3 hours. Shortly before serving, add the fresh sage and parsley to the sauce and mix until well-combined.

COOK ON LOW
4 TO 6 HOURS

CLAMS FLORENTINE

makes 8 servings

A combination of the sea-flavor of clams, the freshness of spinach, and aged Parmesan cheese.

2 6½ oz. cans	chopped clams, drained
10 oz. pkg.	frozen chopped spinach, thawed and well drained
½ cup	Parmesan cheese, grated
½ cup	soft bread crumbs
⅓ cup	yellow onion, chopped
¼ cup	unsalted butter or margarine, melted
1½ cups	half-and-half cream
½ tsp.	salt
½ tsp.	freshly ground black pepper
1 lb.	egg noodles, cooked al denté and drained
	cooking spray

•••*To increase this recipe, double all ingredients and use a
5, 6 or 7-quart Crock-Pot® slow cooker.*

Lightly coat the Crock-Pot® slow cooker with cooking spray. Combine all ingredients, except the noodles, in the stoneware and mix thoroughly. Cover; cook on Low 4 to 6 hours (or on High for 2 to 3 hours). To serve, arrange the noodles in a large serving bowl and ladle the clams and sauce over all.

Corn & Cheese Chowder p. 33

Asian Spiced Chicken Wings p. 24

Wild Mushroom Beef Stew p. 51

Any Day of the Week Beef Chili p. 63

Chicken & Vegetable Lasagna p. 94

Valencian Seafood Paella p. 105

Cheese & Chile Enchilada Casserole p. 136

Hungarian Beef Goulash p. 143

French Onion Soup p. 147

Pulled Pork Sandwiches p. 164

Chicken & Fresh Vegetable Noodle Soup p. 178

Tropical Pork Tenderloin p. 181

Classic Baked Apples p. 203

Candied Bananas Foster p. 216

CHAPTER SIX
Enticing Global Recipes

CHICKEN TORTILLA SOUP

COOK ON LOW
4 TO 6 HOURS

makes 6 servings

Chicken, tortillas, tomatoes, and spices combine to form a hearty Mexican soup that is good for the soul. You can make this soup vegetarian by omitting the chicken and substituting vegetable broth for the chicken broth.

3	boneless, skinless chicken breasts
14 oz. can	diced tomatoes (fire-roasted, if available)
2	jalapeño peppers, seeded and minced
6	corn tortillas, chopped
4 cloves	garlic, minced
1 medium	yellow onion, chopped
1 tsp.	ground cumin
1 tsp.	chili powder
½ tsp.	salt
½ tsp.	freshly ground black pepper
4 cups	chicken broth
1 Tbs.	fresh cilantro, minced
1 large	ripe avocado, diced
6 oz.	crumbly fresh cheese, such as feta
2 cups	tortilla chips, crumbled, for garnish
2	limes, cut into wedges

•••*To increase this recipe, double all ingredients and use a*
5, 6 or 7-quart Crock-Pot® slow cooker.

Place the chicken, tomatoes, peppers, chopped tortillas, garlic, onion, cumin, chili powder, salt, pepper, and chicken broth in the Crock-Pot® slow cooker. Cover; Cook on Low 4 to 6 hours (or on High 2 to 3 hours).

Carefully remove the chicken and, when cool enough to handle, shred using two forks. Place the shredded chicken back into the stoneware and add the cilantro. Ladle the soup into bowls and top with avocado, cheese, and crumbled tortilla chips. Squeeze the juice of a lime wedge over the top of each serving.

INDONESIAN GINGER CHICKEN

makes 4 servings

This entrée easily captures the sweet-salty flavors of Indonesia. Serve over white rice to enjoy all the delicious juices left in the Crock-Pot® slow cooker.

½ cup	honey
¼ cup	soy sauce
1½ Tbs.	fresh ginger, grated
4 cloves	garlic, minced
4	boneless, skinless chicken breasts
1 Tbs.	fresh cilantro, minced

In a small bowl, whisk together the honey, soy sauce, ginger, and garlic. Place the chicken breasts in the Crock-Pot® slow cooker and pour the honey-soy sauce over the chicken. Cover; cook on Low 2 to 3 hours (or on High for 1 hour). Before serving, garnish with a sprinkling of cilantro.

SOUTHEAST ASIAN SEAFOOD STEW

COOK ON LOW
6 TO 8 HOURS

makes 6 servings

The tangy broth of this seafood stew has a fresh, clean taste. Served over jasmine or white rice,
this stew is especially satisfying.

8 oz. can	tomato sauce
1 medium	yellow onion, chopped
1 cup	white wine
1 cup	chicken or vegetable broth
¼ cup	vegetable oil
¼ cup	fresh lime juice
½ cup	fresh coriander or cilantro, chopped
3 medium	tomatoes, cut into small wedges
4 cloves	garlic, minced
2 tsp.	fresh ginger, grated
½ tsp.	red pepper flakes
½ tsp.	cayenne pepper
½ lb.	fresh or frozen cod or other whitefish fillets, thawed and cut into bite-sized pieces
⅓ lb.	fresh prawns, peeled and deveined
⅓ lb.	fresh scallops
½ lb.	fresh mussels or clams
	cilantro sprigs, for garnish
2	limes, cut into wedges

•••To increase this recipe, double the cilantro, tomatoes, garlic, ginger, red pepper,
cayenne pepper, fish and seafood. Do not increase the remaining ingredients.
Use a 5, 6 or 7-quart Crock-Pot® slow cooker.

Combine all ingredients, except for shellfish, limes and cilantro sprigs, in the Crock-Pot® slow cooker. Cover; cook on Low 6 to 8 hours (or on High for 3 to 4 hours). Thirty minutes before serving, add the shellfish to the stoneware and turn to High. Garnish with cilantro sprigs and serve with lime wedges.

COOK ON LOW
6 TO 8 HOURS

CHEESE & CHILE ENCHILADA CASSEROLE

makes 6 servings

Out-of-this-world spicy seasonings meet beef, cheese and all the Mexican fixings for a perfect partnership!

1 large	yellow onion, diced
2 cloves	garlic, minced
1 Tbs.	vegetable oil
2 lbs.	lean ground beef
1.25 oz. pkg.	taco seasoning mix
1 cup	condensed cream of mushroom soup
4 oz. can	diced green chilies
12	corn tortillas
1 cup	Jack cheese, shredded
1 cup	cheddar cheese, shredded
1 cup	sour cream
1 cup	tomatillo salsa (or substitute any mild salsa)
4 oz. can	sliced black olives
¼ cup	green onions, sliced thinly

•••*To increase this recipe, double all ingredients and use a
5, 6 or 7-quart Crock-Pot® slow cooker.*

In a medium skillet, sauté the onion and garlic in the oil. Add the ground beef and brown. Drain the fat from the beef. Add the taco seasoning and mix thoroughly. In a mixing bowl, combine the cream of mushroom soup with the diced green chilies. Spoon 3 tablespoons of the soup mixture into the Crock-Pot® slow cooker and spread to cover the bottom of the stoneware. Create the next layer with 3 tortillas, ¼ cup of the soup mixture, ⅓ of the ground beef mixture, ½ cup of a combination of the cheeses. Continue layering the ingredients until all are used. Do not stir. Cover; cook on Low 6 to 8 hours (or on High for 3 to 4 hours).

In a small mixing bowl, combine the sour cream and tomatillo salsa. Top each serving with the sour cream salsa, a sprinkling of black olives, and a garnish of green onions.

INDONESIAN BEEF RENDANG

COOK ON LOW
8 TO 10 HOURS

makes 6 servings

This traditional beef dish is an example of fusion cooking at its best – Chinese, Indian and Thai flavors combine with sweetness and spice.

2 medium	yellow onions, roughly chopped
3 cloves	garlic, roughly chopped
1 Tbs.	fresh ginger, chopped
4	small red chile peppers, seeded and chopped
½ cup	water
2 lbs.	round steak, cut into 1¼-inch cubes
2 tsp.	ground coriander
1 Tbs.	tamarind paste (substitute 1 Tbs. lime juice)
1 tsp.	ground turmeric
2 tsp.	curry powder
	stem of lemongrass, 4 inches long
2 cups	coconut milk

•••To increase this recipe, double all ingredients except the water and coconut milk and use a 5, 6 or 7-quart Crock-Pot® slow cooker.

In a food processor, blend the onions, garlic, ginger, chili peppers, and water until smooth. Add this mixture, steak and the rest of the ingredients to the Crock-Pot® slow cooker and combine thoroughly. Cover; cook on Low 8 to 10 hours (or on High for 4 to 6 hours).

Halfway through cooking, remove the lid and mix thoroughly to prevent the coconut milk from separating. Replace the cover. Remove the lemongrass before serving.

COOK ON LOW
6 TO 8 HOURS

INDIAN LAMB KORMA

makes 6 servings

A traditional Indian lamb dish that everyone will love! Serve with basmati rice and a side of
Cucumber Raita *for an exotic, yet simple meal.*

2 large	yellow onions, chopped
2 tsp.	fresh ginger, finely grated
3 cloves	garlic, minced
2 large	dried chile peppers, seeded and de-stemmed, finely minced
2 Tbs.	vegetable oil
¾ tsp.	ground turmeric
2 tsp.	ground cumin
1 Tbs.	ground coriander
1½ lbs.	boneless lamb, cut into 1-inch cubes
⅔ cup	ripe tomatoes, chopped
¼ tsp.	ground cloves
½ tsp.	ground cinnamon
¼ tsp.	ground cardamom
¼ tsp.	freshly ground black pepper
½ cup	water
½ cup	heavy cream

•••*To increase this recipe, double all the ingredients except the water and cream.*
Use a 5, 6 or 7-quart Crock-Pot® slow cooker.

In a medium skillet, sauté the onions, ginger, garlic and chilies in the oil. Add the turmeric, cumin and coriander and blend well. Add the lamb, turning the meat as it browns. When browned, spoon the lamb and spices into the Crock-Pot® slow cooker. Add the tomatoes, cloves, cinnamon, cardamom, black pepper and water and mix thoroughly. Cover; cook on Low 6 to 8 hours (or on High for 3 to 4 hours). Thirty minutes before serving, stir in the heavy cream, cover and continue cooking until warmed through.

Cucumber Raita

makes 6 servings

A light touch of minted yogurt and cucumber.

1 large	cucumber, seeded and grated
1 tsp.	salt
½ cup	plain yogurt
2 Tbs.	fresh mint, chopped

In a small bowl, sprinkle the cucumber with salt, and let stand for 5 minutes. Drain off the cucumber liquid. Stir in the yogurt and mint, and serve with the Indian Lamb Korma.

COOK ON LOW
6 TO 8 HOURS

BANGKOK STEAK SALAD

makes 6 servings

This succulent steak salad is best made in the height of summer, when fresh mint, cilantro and basil are at their most fragrant. The slightly sweet peanut vinaigrette is a delicious counterpoint to the robustly flavored flank steak.

Marinade:

2 Tbs.	soy sauce
2 Tbs.	vegetable oil
4 cloves	garlic, minced
1 Tbs.	ginger, grated
1 Tbs.	lemongrass, finely sliced (or 1 Tbs. lemon juice)
1 Tbs.	Asian fish sauce
1 tsp.	Asian chile paste
1½ lbs.	beef flank steak, trimmed of excess fat

Vinaigrette:

2 Tbs.	creamy peanut butter
2 Tbs.	rice wine vinegar
1 Tbs.	fresh lime juice
	salt and pepper to taste

Salad:

1	green cabbage, thinly shredded (or equivalent coleslaw mix)
2 medium	carrots, thinly julienned
½ cup	fresh mint, coarsely chopped
½ cup	fresh cilantro, coarsely chopped
½ cup	fresh basil, coarsely chopped
¼ cup	green onions, finely sliced
¼ cup	unsalted peanuts, toasted and coarsely chopped

•••*To increase this recipe, double all ingredients and use a
5, 6 or 7-quart Crock-Pot® slow cooker.*

In a small mixing bowl, whisk together the soy sauce, vegetable oil, garlic, ginger, lemongrass (or lemon juice), fish sauce, and chile paste. Place the flank steak in the Crock-Pot® slow cooker and pour the sauce over the steak, coating the steak completely with the marinade. Cover and cook on Low 6 to 8 hours (or on High for 3 to 4 hours). Remove the flank steak and reserve ½ cup of the liquid in the stoneware. Let the steak stand 10 minutes before slicing thinly across the grain of the meat.

Assemble the salad vinaigrette by whisking together the reserved stoneware liquid, peanut butter, rice wine vinegar and lime juice. Add salt and pepper to taste. In a large mixing bowl, combine the green cabbage, carrots, mint, cilantro, basil and green onions. Dress with the salad vinaigrette and toss well. Divide the salad onto individual plates, and place slices of steak across each plate. Garnish with a sprinkling of the chopped peanuts.

COOK ON LOW
8 TO 9 HOURS

MILANO MINESTRONE SOUP

makes 6 servings

This substantial Italian classic is a great way to eat your vegetables. Serve with crusty French bread and a green salad for a complete and satisfying meal.

1 cup	smoked ham, diced
1 medium	yellow onion, finely chopped
2 cloves	garlic, minced
2 medium	carrots, diced
2 ribs	celery, diced
2	zucchini squash, diced
1 medium	russet potato, peeled and diced
1 cup	green cabbage, shredded
14½ oz. can	crushed tomatoes, drained
15 oz. can	kidney beans, drained and rinsed
4 cups	vegetable broth
2 Tbs.	dried parsley
1 Tbs.	dried sweet basil
½ cup	elbow macaroni, cooked al denté and drained
	salt to taste

•••*To increase this recipe, double all ingredients and use a 5, 6 or 7-quart Crock-Pot® slow cooker.*

Combine all ingredients, except for the macaroni, in Crock-Pot® slow cooker. Mix thoroughly. Cover; cook on Low 8 to 9 hours (or on High for 3 to 4 hours). Add the macaroni during the last hour of cooking. Add salt to taste.

HUNGARIAN BEEF GOULASH

COOK ON LOW
6 TO 8 HOURS

makes 6 servings

Traditional Hungarian goulash is more like a soup than a stew with gravy. You can serve this as you would find it in Hungary or simply add the sour cream and flour to thicken the juices and form a nicely seasoned gravy. Be sure to serve the more American-style goulash over egg noodles.

1½ lbs.	beef stew meat, cut into 1-inch cubes
½ tsp.	salt
½ tsp.	freshly ground black pepper
2 Tbs.	vegetable oil
3 medium	russet potatoes, cut into 1-inch cubes
1 medium	yellow onion, chopped
2 cloves	garlic, minced
2 medium	red bell peppers, seeded and chopped
2 cups	beef broth
1 tsp.	caraway seeds
3 Tbs.	sweet Hungarian paprika
1 cup	tomato sauce
1 tsp.	kosher salt
½ tsp.	freshly ground black pepper
½ cup	sour cream (optional)
¼ cup	all-purpose flour (optional)

Season the beef cubes with the salt and pepper. In a medium skillet, brown the stew meat in the vegetable oil on medium-high heat, working in batches if necessary. Place the browned meat in the Crock-Pot® slow cooker with the potatoes, onion, garlic, peppers, broth, caraway seeds, paprika, tomato sauce, salt, and pepper. Cover; Cook on Low 6 to 8 hours (or on High 3 to 4 hours).

Serve as a traditional soup or finish in the American style by combining the sour cream and flour. Add to the liquid in the stoneware, stir and cook on High for 5 to 10 minutes, until the sauce has thickened to form a gravy.

COOK ON LOW
6 TO 8 HOURS

THAI GREEN CURRY CHICKEN & BROCCOLI

makes 4 servings

Use the shortcut of curry paste to speed the prep work in this recipe. You'll find the floral aromas of lemongrass, galanga, and lime will quickly transport you to Thailand in no time. The curry paste can be a bit spicy so adjust according to your taste. You can also add your favorite vegetables, such as snap peas, asparagus, or baby corn.
Serve this curry over jasmine rice.

2 Tbs.	green curry paste
1 cup	chicken broth
3	boneless, skinless chicken breasts
3 medium	carrots, cut into ½-inch slices
3 medium	potatoes, cut into 1-inch cubes
20 oz.	unsweetened coconut milk
3 cups	fresh broccoli florets
½ cup	frozen peas
2 Tbs.	fresh lime juice
2 Tbs.	fresh cilantro, minced

•••*To increase this recipe, double all the ingredients except the chicken broth and coconut milk and use a 5, 6 or 7-quart Crock-Pot® slow cooker.*

In a small bowl, whisk together the curry paste and chicken broth until blended. Place the chicken, carrots, and potatoes into the Crock-Pot® slow cooker. Pour the green curry chicken broth over the chicken and vegetables. Cover; cook on Low 6 to 8 hours (or on High 3 to 4 hours). In the last hour of cooking, add the coconut milk and broccoli florets, mixing lightly. Five minutes before serving, shred the chicken using two forks and return to the stoneware. Add the peas and stir. Continue cooking for 5 minutes. Before serving, top with fresh lime juice and cilantro.

Hearty Black Bean Soup

makes 8 servings

This rich soup has an earthy sweetness that is hard to resist. Serve with tortilla chips and lime wedges for an extra dimension.

1 lb.	black beans, soaked overnight and drained
2 Tbs.	vegetable oil
1 large	yellow onion, finely chopped
2 cloves	garlic, minced
2 Tbs.	fresh cilantro or Italian parsley, minced
2 quarts	chicken or vegetable broth
¼ cup	crumbly fresh cheese, such as feta cheese

•••*To increase this recipe, double all ingredients except the chicken broth and use a 5, 6 or 7-quart Crock-Pot® slow cooker.*

Combine all ingredients, except the cheese, in the Crock-Pot® slow cooker. Cover; cook on High 2 hours, then on Low 8-10 hours. To assemble, sprinkle the cheese evenly in eight individual bowls and pour the soup over the cheese.

COOK ON LOW
10 TO 12 HOURS

NIKU JAGA

makes 6 servings

A delicious Japanese beef one-dish meal. Serve with sticky white rice on the side.

2 lbs.	beef stew meat, cut in 1-inch cubes
1 cup	water
½ cup	Japanese sake (or dry white wine)
¼ cup	sugar
¼ cup	soy sauce
1 tsp.	salt
4 medium	carrots, sliced on the bias
3 medium	russet potatoes, peeled and chopped
1	white onion, chopped

•••*To increase this recipe, double all ingredients and use a
5, 6 or 7-quart Crock-Pot® slow cooker.*

Combine all the ingredients in the Crock-Pot® slow cooker. Cover; cook on Low 10 to 12 hours (or on High for 4 to 6 hours). Stir stew thoroughly before serving.

French Onion Soup

makes 6 servings

The cheese and bread croutons accent the subtle, buttery flavor of this soup, while the chives give it a splash of color.

4 large	yellow onions, diced
½ cup	butter or margarine
2 Tbs.	flour
6 cups	beef broth
1 tsp.	salt
6 thick	slices baguette, toasted
1 cup	Gruyère cheese, shredded
1 Tbs.	fresh chives, finely chopped, as garnish

•••*To increase this recipe, double all ingredients and use a
5, 6 or 7-quart Crock-Pot® slow cooker.*

In a large skillet, sauté the onions in the butter. Add the flour and mix thoroughly. Add the onion mixture to the Crock-Pot® slow cooker. Add the beef broth and salt. Cover; cook on Low 8 to 10 hours (or on High for 4 to 5 hours).

Ladle the soup into six ovenproof bowls. Turn on the broiler. Scatter the cheese evenly on the baguette slices and float one piece of bread on top of each serving of soup. Broil until the cheese is melted, about 3 to 4 minutes. Sprinkle with fresh chives and serve at once.

COOK ON LOW
4 TO 6 HOURS

VICHYSSOISE

makes 6 servings

*Traditionally, this smooth and creamy soup is served chilled, but it is equally delicious when served warm.
It is a beautiful first course for an elegant meal.*

2 large	leeks, chopped
2 medium	potatoes, peeled and chopped
3 cups	chicken broth
2 Tbs.	chives, chopped
1 cup	milk
½ cup	heavy cream
	grated nutmeg, for garnish

•••*To increase this recipe, double all ingredients and use a
5, 6 or 7-quart Crock-Pot® slow cooker.*

Combine the leeks, potatoes, chicken broth and chives in the Crock-Pot® slow cooker. Cover; cook on Low 4 to 6 hours (or on High for 2 to 3 hours). After cooking, add the milk and allow the soup to cool.

Place the soup in a food processor or blender, working in batches. Puree each batch for 1 minute or until smooth. Transfer to a large serving bowl and add the cream. Stir thoroughly. Serve at room temperature or refrigerate for up to 2 days. Garnish with the nutmeg before serving.

CARNITAS

COOK ON LOW
8 TO 10 HOURS

makes 6 servings

Crispy and indulgent, this Mexican pork dish has hints of citrusy sweetness with a bit of kick. Serve the carnitas with Mexican rice, beans, and tortillas, or as a filling for tacos or burritos.

2½ lbs.	pork butt roast, trimmed of excess fat
1 tsp.	kosher salt
1 tsp.	garlic powder
1 tsp.	chili powder
1 tsp.	dried oregano
1 tsp.	black pepper
1 cup	cola
1	orange, peeled and cut into slices

Season the pork roast with the dry spices. Place in a self-sealing plastic bag and marinate overnight. Place the marinated pork roast in the Crock-Pot® slow cooker. Pour the cola over the pork and cover the roast with the orange slices. Cover; cook on Low 8 to 10 hours (or on High 4 to 6 hours).

Remove the roast and shred with two forks. Place the shredded pork on a large baking sheet and bake at 425°F for 25 minutes, or until the pork becomes crispy. Sprinkle some of the leftover juices from the stoneware over the pork and serve right away.

COOK ON LOW
6 TO 8 HOURS

POSOLE

makes 6 servings

This classic Mexican stew can be made with pork or chicken, so try both!

1 lb.	boneless pork loin roast or 2 boneless, skinless chicken breasts
1 medium	yellow onion, chopped
2½ cups	broth (beef or chicken)
2 15 oz. cans	hominy, drained
2 4 oz. cans	diced green fire-roasted chiles
3 cloves	garlic, sliced
1½ Tbs.	chili powder
1 tsp.	ground cumin
1 tsp.	salt
½ tsp.	freshly ground black pepper
½ tsp.	dried oregano
2 Tbs.	fresh cilantro, minced

Place all of the ingredients except the cilantro in the Crock-Pot® slow cooker. Cover; cook on Low 6 to 8 hours (or on High 3 to 4 hours). Remove the pork or chicken from the stoneware and shred the meat with two forks. Place the shredded meat back into the stoneware and add the fresh cilantro right before serving.

TAQUERIA-STYLE CHICKEN SOFT TACOS

COOK ON LOW
6 TO 8 HOURS

makes 4 servings

Taquerias, which are Mexican taco stands, specialize in intensely flavored meats on soft corn tortillas, topped with chopped white onion, cilantro, and salsa. This chicken recipe is definitely part of that tradition. Other taco toppings include shredded cheese, shredded lettuce, chopped tomato, and sour cream.
Serve the tacos with rice and beans.

3½ to 4 lbs.	broiler/fryer chicken, cleaned and patted dry
1 tsp.	kosher salt
½ tsp.	freshly ground black pepper
1 tsp.	dried oregano
2 tsp.	chili powder
1 head	garlic, cut in half
2	limes, cut into quarters
½ bunch	cilantro, stems removed
12 8-inch	corn or flour tortillas
1 medium	white onion, finely chopped
3 ripe	avocados, chopped
¼ cup	fresh cilantro, chopped
	hot pepper sauce or your favorite salsa
2	limes, quartered

Season the inner and outer surfaces of the chicken with the salt, pepper, oregano, and chili powder. Place the garlic halves, lime quarters, and cilantro into the cavity of the chicken. Place the chicken, breast side up, in the Crock-Pot® slow cooker. Cover; cook on Low 6 to 8 hours. Remove the chicken, discard the skin and remove the meat from the bones. Discard the bones. Shred the chicken meat with two forks and place in a bowl. Add ½ cup of the juices from the stoneware, mixing to combine.

Heat the tortillas in the microwave or on the stovetop until warm and pliable. On each heated tortilla, place about 1/8 cup of shredded chicken. Top with a sprinkling of white onion, avocado, and cilantro. Season with hot pepper sauce or your favorite salsa and a squeeze of lime.

WHITE BEAN & SAUSAGE CASSOULET

makes 6 servings

This homey, charming dish is typical fare in the bistros of France and for good reason. It is full of enough warmth and heartiness to heat up one's soul a cold winter night. Serve with crusty bread and a green salad dressed with a mustard vinaigrette.

1 lb.	Great Northern or cannellini beans, soaked overnight and drained
6 cups	water
1 medium	white onion, chopped
¼ cup	dark molasses
15 oz. can	tomato sauce
2 tsp.	Dijon mustard
1 tsp.	kosher salt
1 tsp.	dried thyme
½ tsp.	freshly ground black pepper
1 Tbs.	Worcestershire sauce
3 medium	carrots, cut into 1-inch slices
1 lb.	smoked sausage, such as kielbasa, cut into 1-inch slices
2 tsp.	cornstarch

Place the beans in the Crock-Pot® slow cooker and cover with 6 cups water. Cover; cook on High for 2 hours. Drain the beans, reserving the cooking liquid. Place the beans and the remaining ingredients in the stoneware and add 2 cups of the reserved cooking liquid. Mix well to combine. Cover; cook on Low 8 to 10 hours.

During the last 15 minutes of cooking, whisk the cornstarch with 2 tablespoons of water and add to the cassoulet. Stir and cook until thickened.

KINPURA GOBO

makes 4 servings

A Japanese childhood favorite, this recipe combines the nutritional benefits of burdock root (known in Japan as "gobo") with sweet and salty flavors imparted by the soy sauce and sugar. For variation, try adding lotus root or sweet potato. Burdock root can be found in Asian specialty markets or natural food stores.

1 lb.	ground beef
2 medium	burdock roots, peeled and julienned
2 medium	carrots, peeled and julienned
14 oz. can	black beans, rinsed and drained
2 Tbs.	sesame oil
¼ cup	sake or dry white wine
3 Tbs.	sugar
¼ cup	soy sauce
2 cups	dashi or water

•••*To increase this recipe, double all ingredients and use a
5, 6 or 7-quart Crock-Pot® slow cooker.*

In a medium skillet, brown the ground beef and drain off any excess fat. Transfer the ground beef to the Crock-Pot® slow cooker and add the remaining ingredients, mixing thoroughly. Cover; cook on Low 8 to 10 hours (or on High for 4 to 5 hours).

COOK ON HIGH
1 HOUR & LOW
7 TO 9 HOURS

ARROZ CON POLLO

makes 4 servings

Many Latin American countries have their own version of this traditional Spanish dish.
This main entrée owes its vibrant yellow color to the saffron.

pinch	saffron
2 Tbs.	boiling water
1 large	yellow onion, chopped
2 cloves	garlic, minced
1	green bell pepper, seeded and chopped
1 cup	converted, long-grain rice
1 Tbs.	vegetable oil
2 whole	bay leaves
1 tsp.	dried oregano
½ tsp.	ground paprika
1 tsp.	salt
½ tsp.	freshly ground pepper
14 oz. can	plum tomatoes, drained and chopped
8	boneless chicken thighs
	salt and pepper to taste
1½ cups	lowfat, low-sodium chicken broth
1 cup	frozen peas, defrosted

•••*To increase this recipe, double all ingredients and use a*
5, 6 or 7-quart Crock-Pot® slow cooker.

In a small bowl, combine the saffron and boiling water and set aside. In a large skillet, sauté the onion, garlic, pepper and rice in the vegetable oil. Season with the bay leaves, oregano, paprika, salt and pepper. Add the plum tomatoes and stir well. Transfer the vegetable and rice mixture to the Crock-Pot® slow cooker.

Season the chicken thighs with salt and pepper. In the same skillet, sauté the chicken thighs until browned. Place the chicken thighs on top of the rice layer in the stoneware. Add the saffron and water, and the chicken broth. Cover; cook on High for 1 hour, then reduce to Low for 7 to 9 hours. Thirty minutes before the end of cooking, add the frozen peas and mix the contents thoroughly. Remove the bay leaves before serving.

CLASSIC ITALIAN BEEF SPAGHETTI

COOK ON LOW
6 TO 8 HOURS

makes 6 servings

A hearty meal best served with a sprinkling of freshly grated Parmesan cheese and a basket full of garlic bread.

1	medium onion, chopped
2 cloves	garlic, minced
1	green bell pepper, seeded and diced
1 rib	celery, sliced
1½ lbs.	ground beef
1	medium carrot, diced
6	mushrooms, sliced
2 8 oz. cans	tomato sauce
1½ cups	water
14 oz. can	stewed tomatoes, chopped, including liquid
2 tsp.	fresh oregano, minced
1 tsp.	Italian parsley, minced
1½ tsp.	salt
1 tsp.	freshly ground black pepper
2 tsp.	sugar
8 oz.	dry spaghetti, broken into thirds

*•••To increase this recipe, double all ingredients and use a
5, 6 or 7-quart Crock-Pot® slow cooker.*

In a medium skillet, sauté the onion, garlic, green pepper and celery. Add the beef and brown. Drain any grease and pour the beef and vegetables into the Crock-Pot® slow cooker. Add the carrot, mushrooms, tomato sauce, water, stewed tomatoes with the liquid, oregano, parsley, salt, pepper and sugar. Cover; cook on Low 6 to 8 hours (or on High for 3 to 5 hours). One hour before serving, turn to High and stir in the dry spaghetti. Cover and cook until the noodles are tender.

COOK ON LOW
7 TO 9 HOURS

ROPA VIEJA

makes 4 servings

Serve with warm tortillas to scoop up the savory meat, vegetables and pan juices.

1½ lbs.	flank steak, trimmed of excess fat
2 large	carrots, cut into 1-inch slices
1 cup	vegetable broth
1 large	white onion, diced
2 cloves	garlic, minced
1	green bell pepper, seeded and chopped
½ tsp.	cayenne pepper
1 tsp.	salt
1 tsp.	freshly ground black pepper
2 large	tomatoes, chopped
2	jalapeño peppers, seeded and minced
2 Tbs.	tomato paste

•••*To increase this recipe, double all the ingredients except the broth. Increase the broth to 1½ cups. Use a 5, 6 or 7-quart Crock-Pot® slow cooker.*

Place the flank steak, carrots and vegetable broth in the Crock-Pot® slow cooker. Cover; cook on Low 7 to 9 hours (or on High for 3½ to 4½ hours). Remove the flank steak and carrots from the stoneware and shred the steak. Set aside. Reserve 1½ cups of the juices from the stoneware.

In a large pan, sauté the onion, garlic, and green pepper until soft. Season with the cayenne pepper, salt, and black pepper. Add the tomatoes, jalapeños, and tomato paste to the pan, plus the 1½ cups of the reserved cooking juices. Bring to a boil and lower to a simmer, covered, for 20 minutes. During the last 5 minutes of simmering, uncover the pan and let the sauce reduce. Pour the sauce over individual servings of the carrots and shredded beef.

CHAPTER SEVEN

5+5 Recipes: Five-Minute Prep & Five Easy Ingredients

Note: Certain basic pantry items, such as salt and pepper, are assumed to be on hand for all cooks and have not been included in the "five ingredient" count.

PORK CHILE VERDE

makes 6 servings

COOK ON LOW
6 TO 8 HOURS

Serve this deliciously easy dish with Mexican-style rice and tortillas.

2 tsp.	kosher salt
1 tsp.	ground cumin
1 tsp.	garlic powder
1 tsp.	freshly ground black pepper
2½ lbs.	boneless pork roast, trimmed of excess fat, cut into 1-inch cubes
16 oz. jar	salsa verde

•••*To increase this recipe, double all ingredients and use a
5, 6 or 7-quart Crock-Pot® slow cooker.*

In a small bowl, combine the salt, cumin, garlic powder, and pepper. Season the pork with this mixture and place in the Crock-Pot® slow cooker. Add the salsa verde and mix well to combine. Cover; cook on Low 6 to 8 hours (or on High 3 to 4 hours). Spoon the sauce over the pork to serve.

PENNE WITH THREE CHEESES

makes 6 servings

An elegant variation of macaroni and cheese. Use your favorite pre-shredded cheese blend to speed your prep time.

10 oz. container	refrigerated Alfredo sauce
1 cup	milk
12 oz. can	evaporated milk
4 cups	shredded Italian 3 cheese blend
1 lb.	penne pasta, uncooked
1 tsp.	kosher salt
½ tsp.	freshly ground black pepper
	cooking spray

•••*To increase this recipe, double all ingredients and use a
5, 6 or 7-quart Crock-Pot® slow cooker.*

Lightly coat the Crock-Pot® slow cooker with cooking spray. In a medium bowl, whisk together the alfredo sauce, milk, and evaporated milk until very smooth. Pour into the Crock-Pot® slow cooker and add the remaining ingredients. Mix well to combine. Cover; cook on Low 3 to 4 hours. Do not remove the cover or mix while cooking.

CHEESE TORTELLINI WITH MEATBALLS

COOK ON LOW
8 TO 10 HOURS

makes 4 servings

Take advantage of your grocery store specials to create shortcuts for your meals. This recipe uses prepared ingredients to produce a delicious entrée with homemade taste.

24 oz.	frozen prepared meatballs
26 oz. jar	tomato basil pasta sauce
1½ cups	shredded Italian cheese blend
9 oz. pkg.	refrigerated cheese tortellini
¼ cup	fresh basil leaves, chopped

•••*To increase this recipe, double all ingredients and use a
5, 6 or 7-quart Crock-Pot® slow cooker.*

Combine the meatballs, pasta sauce and cheese in the Crock-Pot® slow cooker. Mix well with a large spoon. Cover; cook on Low 8 to 10 hours. In the last hour of cooking, add the tortellini, mixing again lightly. Cover and continue cooking. Before serving, mix in the fresh basil leaves.

COOK ON LOW
3 TO 4 HOURS

CHICKEN CHILAQUILES

makes 6 servings

Originally created in Mexico to use up leftover chicken and tortillas, this quick-prep recipe delivers fantastic flavor. Garnish each serving with a dollop of sour cream, if desired, and serve over white rice.

10¾ oz. can	condensed cream of chicken soup
½ cup	water
4	boneless, skinless chicken breasts, cut into bite-sized pieces
1 cup	cheddar cheese, shredded
7 oz. can	chopped green chiles
3 cups	tortilla chips, roughly crumbled

•••*To increase this recipe, double all ingredients and use a 5, 6 or 7-quart Crock-Pot® slow cooker.*

In a small bowl, whisk together the soup and water. Place the chicken, cheese, and green chiles in the Crock-Pot® slow cooker and add the soup, mixing well to combine. Cover; cook on Low 3 to 4 hours (or on High for 2 hours). Add the tortilla chips in the last 15 minutes of cooking and stir to combine. Cover and continue cooking until done.

Split Pea Soup

makes 8 servings

Homemade, hearty soup–ready when you are.

Cook on Low
8 to 10 hours

2 cups	split peas, cleaned
6 cups	chicken broth
2	meaty ham hocks
2 cups	prepared diced carrots and onions (found in the produce section)
1 tsp.	salt
1 tsp.	finely ground black pepper

•••To increase this recipe, double all ingredients and use a 5, 6 or 7-quart Crock-Pot® slow cooker.

Place all of the ingredients in the Crock-Pot® slow cooker, mixing to combine. Cover; cook on Low 8 to 10 hours (or on High 4 to 5 hours). Remove the ham hocks from the soup. Using an immersion blender or potato masher, mash some of the peas (this helps thicken the soup). Return the mashed peas to the soup. Remove the meat from the ham hocks and return to the soup. Stir well and re-heat the soup briefly on High, if needed.

COOK ON LOW
8 TO 10 HOURS

PULLED PORK SANDWICHES

makes 8 servings

Always a family hit!

2½ lbs.	boneless pork roast
½ tsp.	kosher salt
½ tsp.	freshly ground black pepper
18 oz. jar	your favorite barbecue sauce
⅔ cup	mayonnaise
8	sandwich buns, split and toasted
16 slices	sweet pickle

•••*To increase this recipe, double all ingredients and use a
5, 6 or 7-quart Crock-Pot® slow cooker.*

Season the roast with salt and pepper. Place in the Crock-Pot® slow cooker and cover with the barbecue sauce. Cover; cook on Low 8 to 10 hours (or on High 4 to 6 hours). Cool slightly and shred the pork roast using two forks. Mix the sauce with the meat.

To assemble the sandwiches, spread the mayonnaise on the buns and pile the pulled pork on top. Top each sandwich with two slices of pickle and serve at once.

BARBECUE BABY BACK RIBS

COOK ON LOW
8 TO 10 HOURS

makes 4 servings

The intense flavor of barbecue doesn't have to come from the grill! This recipe creates fall-off-the-bone tender and sweet baby back ribs.

2 Tbs.	dark brown sugar
2 tsp.	smoked ground paprika
1 tsp.	chili powder
1 tsp.	salt
1 tsp.	freshly ground black pepper
2½ lbs.	pork baby back ribs
¼ cup	your favorite smoky barbecue sauce

•••To increase this recipe, double all ingredients and use a 5, 6 or 7-quart Crock-Pot® slow cooker.

In a small bowl, combine the sugar, paprika, chili powder, salt, and pepper. Spread the spice mixture all over the ribs, covering the entire surface. Place the ribs in the Crock-Pot® slow cooker. Cover; cook on Low 8 to 10 hours. In the last 30 minutes of cooking, brush the ribs with the barbecue sauce. Cover and continue cooking until done.

PESTO LEMON SALMON FILLETS

makes 4 servings

Pesto sauce and lemon make perfect partners for salmon. Serve with a wild rice blend to complement the fish.

1	lemon
½ cup	prepared pesto sauce
½ tsp.	salt
½ tsp.	freshly ground black pepper
4 6 oz.	salmon fillets
	cooking spray

•••*To increase this recipe, double all ingredients and use a
5, 6 or 7-quart Crock-Pot® slow cooker.*

Lightly coat the Crock-Pot® slow cooker with cooking spray. Cut the lemon in half. Slice one half of the lemon into thin slices and reserve. Squeeze the juice of the other lemon half into a small bowl and blend with the pesto, salt, and pepper. Whisk to combine. Place the salmon in the stoneware and cover the fillets with the pesto mixture. Top each fillet with lemon slices. Cover; cook on Low 2 to 3 hours.

MOROCCAN CHICKEN COUSCOUS

COOK ON LOW
4 TO 6 HOURS

makes 4 servings

The warm flavors of North Africa are the stars of this easy chicken dish. Serve this one-dish meal with flatbread.

3 medium	carrots, cut into 1-inch slices
4	boneless, skinless chicken breasts
1 tsp.	kosher salt
½ tsp.	freshly ground black pepper
1	lemon, thinly sliced
½ cup	water
1 cup	pre-cooked couscous pasta
2 Tbs.	fresh mint, chopped

*•••To increase this recipe, double all ingredients and use a
5, 6 or 7-quart Crock-Pot® slow cooker.*

Place the carrots in the bottom of the Crock-Pot® slow cooker. Season the chicken with the salt and pepper. Place on top of the carrots. Place the lemon slices on the chicken breasts and add the water. Cover; cook on Low 4 to 6 hours (or on High 2 to 3 hours).

In the last 10 minutes of cooking, add the couscous and replace the cover. Before serving, top with the fresh mint.

SWEET & SPICY KIELBASA

makes 6 servings

Substitute your favorite smoked sausage for the kielbasa in this sassy, hearty dinner.

½ cup	dark brown sugar
½ cup	grape jelly
2 Tbs.	Dijon mustard
2 lbs.	fully cooked, smoked kielbasa, cut into 1-inch slices
4 medium	potatoes, chopped into 1-inch chunks

•••*To increase this recipe, double all ingredients and use a
5, 6 or 7-quart Crock-Pot® slow cooker.*

In a small bowl, combine the brown sugar, jelly, and mustard. Place the kielbasa slices and potato in the Crock-Pot® slow cooker. Add the brown sugar mixture, coating the kielbasa and potatoes completely. Cover; cook on Low 6 to 8 hours (or on High 3 to 4 hours).

CLASSIC BAKED BEANS

makes 6 servings

Salty with a hint of sweetness, these baked beans are a quick-prep masterpiece.

3 16 oz. cans	pork and beans
¼ cup	dark molasses
½ cup	ketchup
¼ tsp.	dry mustard
½ tsp.	freshly ground black pepper
1 Tbs.	Worcestershire sauce

•••*To increase this recipe, double all ingredients and use a
5, 6 or 7-quart Crock Pot® slow cooker.*

Place all of the ingredients in the Crock-Pot® slow cooker, mixing to combine. Cover; cook on Low 8 to 10 hours (or on High 4 to 5 hours).

COOK ON LOW
4 TO 5 HOURS

CHERRY WALNUT PORK CHOPS

makes 4 servings

Even though this recipe takes only 5 minutes of prep time, this dish is definitely worthy of dinner guests!

4 center-cut	boneless pork chops, 1-inch thick
½ tsp.	kosher salt
½ tsp.	freshly ground black pepper
1 tsp.	low-sodium chicken bouillon granules
21 oz. can	cherry pie filling
2 tsp.	lemon juice
½ cup	walnuts, chopped and toasted

•••*To increase this recipe, double all ingredients and use a
5, 6 or 7-quart Crock-Pot® slow cooker.*

Season the pork chops with the salt and pepper. Place in the Crock-Pot® slow cooker. In a medium bowl, combine the bouillon, pie filling, and lemon juice. Pour over the chops. Cover; cook on Low 4 to 5 hours (or on High 2 to 3 hours).

Remove the chops and place on serving platter. Spoon the cherry sauce over the chops and garnish each chop with the toasted walnuts.

CREAMY DIJON CHICKEN

makes 4 servings

COOK ON LOW
4 HOURS

A soothing winter entrée – perfect for the end of a hectic day of work, soccer practice and household chores.
Steam red potatoes or prepare quick-cooking brown rice as an accompaniment.

10¾ oz. can	condensed cream of chicken soup
3½ Tbs.	Dijon mustard
1 Tbs.	cornstarch
½ tsp.	freshly ground black pepper
½ cup	water
4	boneless, skinless chicken breasts

•••*To increase this recipe, double all ingredients and use a*
5, 6 or 7-quart Crock-Pot® slow cooker.

In a medium bowl, whisk together the soup, mustard, cornstarch, pepper, and water until smooth. Place the chicken breasts in the Crock-Pot® slow cooker and cover with the Dijon sauce. Cover; cook on Low for 4 hours (or on High for 2 hours).

COOK ON LOW
4 TO 6 HOURS

HONEY APRICOT CHICKEN

makes 4 servings

Honey and apricots add sweet flavor and appealing texture to this simple chicken entrée.

½ cup	honey
⅓ cup	chicken broth
1 tsp.	dried mustard
½ tsp.	kosher salt
½ tsp.	freshly ground black pepper
4	boneless, skinless chicken breasts
1 cup	dried apricots, chopped

•••*To increase this recipe, double all ingredients and use a
5, 6 or 7-quart Crock-Pot® slow cooker.*

In a small bowl, whisk together the honey, chicken broth, dried mustard, salt, and pepper. Place the chicken and apricots in the Crock-Pot® slow cooker and pour the honey mixture on top. Cover; cook on Low 4 to 6 hours (or on High 2 to 3 hours).

Alfredo Green Beans with Pancetta

Cook on High
3 to 4 hours

makes 8 servings

Remember everyone's favorite green bean casserole? Your family and friends will love this updated, sophisticated variation.

28 oz. pkg.	frozen, cut green beans
6 oz.	pancetta, crisped in the microwave and chopped
1 cup	roasted red bell peppers, finely chopped
10 oz. container	cheesy alfredo sauce
½ tsp.	freshly ground black pepper
2.5 oz. can	French fried onions

•••*To increase this recipe, double all ingredients and use a 5, 6 or 7-quart Crock-Pot® slow cooker.*

In the Crock-Pot® slow cooker, place the green beans, crispy pancetta, chopped peppers, alfredo sauce, and black pepper, mixing well to combine. Cover; cook on High 3 to 4 hours, stirring once after 1 hour. Just before serving, add the fried onions and stir lightly.

CHAPTER EIGHT

Healthy Balance Recipes: Good-for-You Choices

HEARTY CARROT SOUP

makes 4 servings

COOK ON LOW
6 TO 8 HOURS

*This dish is a great year-round accompaniment to a main course of broiled chicken or fish.
Or, the soup can stand alone as a quick, but satisfying meal in its own right.*

1 medium	leek, thinly sliced
4 medium	parsnips, peeled and diced
4 medium	carrots, peeled and diced
4 cups	nonfat chicken broth
1	bay leaf
½ tsp.	salt
½ tsp.	freshly ground pepper
½ cup	small pasta, cooked al denté and drained
1 Tbs.	Italian parsley, chopped
1 cup	lowfat croutons

•••*To increase this recipe, double all ingredients and use a
5, 6 or 7 quart Crock-Pot® slow cooker.*

In a small skillet, sauté the leek until golden. Drain and place in the Crock-Pot® slow cooker. Add the remaining ingredients, except the pasta, parsley and croutons. Cover; cook on Low 6 to 8 hours or until the vegetables are tender (or on High for 2 to 4 hours). Add the pasta during the last hour of cooking. Sprinkle each individual serving with a garnish of parsley and croutons.

CALORIES 135, FAT 2g (Sat 0g), CARBOHYDRATE 27g, FIBER 7g,
PROTEIN 4g, SODIUM 991mg, CHOLESTEROL 0mg

COOK ON LOW
6 TO 8 HOURS

CHICKEN & FRESH VEGETABLE NOODLE SOUP

makes 4 to 6 servings

Grandma's cure-all for the sniffles, this chicken noodle soup is chock full of fresh vegetables to give you a solid, nutritious boost!

2 medium	onions, chopped
3 medium	carrots, sliced
2 ribs	celery, sliced
2-3 lbs.	whole fryer chicken, cleaned
1 cup	wide egg noodles, cooked al denté and drained
2 Tbs.	dried parsley
1 tsp.	salt
¼ tsp.	freshly ground black pepper
4 cups	chicken broth
1 Tbs.	fresh Italian parsley, minced
2 Tbs.	fresh lemon juice

•••To increase this recipe, double all ingredients and use a 5, 6 or 7-quart Crock-Pot® slow cooker.

Combine all ingredients, except the Italian parsley and lemon juice, in the Crock-Pot® slow cooker. Cover; cook on Low 6 to 8 hours (or on High for 2 to 3 hours). Remove the chicken from the stoneware and let cool slightly.

Remove the chicken meat from the skin and bones and return the meat to the stoneware. Discard the skin and bones. Cover; cook on High for 30 minutes. Skim any fat from the top of the soup. Shortly before serving, add the Italian parsley and fresh lemon juice.

CALORIES 228, FAT 6g (Sat 2g), CARBOHYDRATE 17g, FIBER 3g,
PROTEIN 24g, SODIUM 904mg, CHOLESTEROL 69mg

TURKEY LENTIL SOUP

COOK ON LOW
8 TO 10 HOURS

makes 4 to 6 servings

Turkey bacon has come a long way in mimicking the delicious smoky flavor of bacon without adding the fat.
It imparts a hearty flavor to this protein-rich soup.

1 medium	onion, finely chopped
2 medium	carrots, finely chopped
2 ribs	celery, finely chopped
1 Tbs.	extra-virgin olive oil
8 oz.	smoked turkey bacon, finely chopped
1½ cups	lentils, rinsed
3 cloves	garlic, minced
1 tsp.	salt
1 tsp.	freshly ground black pepper
6 cups	chicken broth

•••*To increase this recipe, double all ingredients and use a*
5, 6 or 7 quart Crock-Pot® slow cooker.

In a medium skillet, sauté the onion, carrots, and celery in the olive oil on medium-high heat until softened, about 7 minutes. Combine the vegetables and oil with the remaining ingredients in the Crock-Pot® slow cooker. Cover; cook on Low 8 to 10 hours (or on High for 4 to 5 hours), or until lentils are tender.

CALORIES 194, FAT 8g (Sat 2g), CARBOHYDRATE 16g, FIBER 5g,
PROTEIN 11g, SODIUM 1656 mg, CHOLESTEROL 27

COOK ON LOW
2 TO 3 HOURS

POACHED LEMON SALMON WITH DILL

makes 4 servings

Salmon is full of important omega-three fats. Serve with steamed fresh vegetables to add color and healthful nutrients to your meal.

4 6 oz.	salmon fillets
½ tsp.	kosher salt
½ tsp.	freshly ground black pepper
2 Tbs.	fresh dill, finely chopped
1	lemon, thinly sliced
¼ cup	dry white wine

Season the salmon with the salt and pepper. Sprinkle the dill over the salmon and place slices of lemon on top of each dill-covered fillet. Place the fillets in the Crock-Pot® slow cooker and add the wine. Cover; cook on Low 2 to 3 hours.

CALORIES 337, FAT 12g (Sat 0g), CARBOHYDRATE 0g, FIBER 0g,
PROTEIN 48g, SODIUM 235mg, CHOLESTEROL 96mg

TROPICAL PORK TENDERLOIN

makes 4 to 6 servings

Pork tenderloin is a protein-packed cut of meat and its mild flavor is well accented by the sweetness of mango and pineapple.

2 1 lb.	pork tenderloins
1 tsp.	kosher salt
½ tsp.	freshly ground black pepper
1 tsp.	ground cumin
1 cup	frozen sliced mango
1 cup	pineapple chunks
3 Tbs.	jalapeño jelly

•••*To increase this recipe, double all ingredients and use a 5, 6 or 7-quart Crock-Pot® slow cooker.*

Season the pork tenderloins with the salt, black pepper and cumin. Place the mango slices and pineapple in the bottom of the Crock-Pot® slow cooker and mix with the jelly. Arrange the tenderloins on top. Cover; cook on Low 6 to 8 hours. Remove the pork tenderloins from the stoneware and use a potato masher to mash together the fruit mixture to form a sauce. Slice the tenderloins and pour the sauce over the slices.

CALORIES 254, FAT 8g (Sat 3g), CARBOHYDRATE 14g, FIBER <1g, PROTEIN 53g, SODIUM 394mg, CHOLESTEROL 100mg

COOK ON LOW
6 TO 8 HOURS

CHICKEN BREASTS WITH WILD MUSHROOMS

makes 6 servings

This rich and elegant dish is surprisingly also good for you.

6	skinless, boneless chicken breasts
1 tsp.	fresh lemon juice
1 tsp.	freshly ground black pepper
1 tsp.	salt
1 tsp.	garlic powder
10¾ oz. can	fat-free cream of chicken soup
10¾ oz. can	fat-free cream of mushroom soup
8	crimini mushrooms, sliced
2	shiitake mushrooms, sliced
2 Tbs.	dried porcini mushrooms
1 Tbs.	fresh Italian parsley, minced
1 clove	garlic, minced
16 oz. pkg.	eggless noodles, cooked al denté and drained

•••*To increase this recipe, double all ingredients except the soups and use a*
5, 6 or 7-quart Crock-Pot® slow cooker.

Season the chicken breasts with the lemon juice, pepper, salt and garlic powder. Place in the Crock-Pot® slow cooker. In a medium mixing bowl, combine the soups, mushrooms, parsley and garlic. Pour the sauce over the chicken breasts. Cover; cook on Low 6 to 8 hours (or on High for 3 to 4 hours). Serve each chicken breast over a bed of noodles, with the sauce ladled generously on top.

CALORIES 434, FAT 8g (Sat 3g), CARBOHYDRATE 32g, FIBER 2g,
PROTEIN 33g, SODIUM 1091mg, CHOLESTEROL 97mg

Cajun Chicken & Shrimp Creole

makes 6 servings

Enjoy the full flavors of chicken, shrimp and spices in this delicious Creole one-dish dinner!

2 lbs.	skinless chicken thighs
1	red bell pepper, chopped
1 large	onion, chopped
2 ribs	celery, diced
15 oz. can	stewed tomatoes with liquid, chopped
3 cloves	garlic, minced
1 Tbs.	granulated sugar
1 tsp.	ground paprika
1 tsp.	Cajun seasoning
1 tsp.	salt
1 tsp.	freshly ground black pepper
1 lb.	shelled shrimp, deveined and cleaned
1 Tbs.	fresh lemon juice
	Louisiana hot sauce to taste
2 cups	prepared quick-cooking brown rice

*•••To increase this recipe, double all ingredients and use a
5, 6 or 7-quart Crock-Pot® slow cooker.*

Place the chicken thighs in the bottom of the Crock-Pot® slow cooker. Add the remaining ingredients except the shrimp, lemon juice, hot sauce and rice. Cover; cook on Low 8 to 10 hours (or on High for 4 to 5 hours). In the last thirty minutes of cooking, add the shrimp, lemon juice and hot sauce. Continue cooking until the shrimp are cooked throughout. Serve over hot brown rice.

CALORIES 352, FAT 12g (Sat 4g), CARBOHYDRATE 25g, FIBER 2g,
PROTEIN 34g, SODIUM 682mg, CHOLESTEROL 142mg

COOK ON LOW
2 TO 3 HOURS

HALIBUT WITH TOMATO LIME TAPENADE

makes 6 servings

A zesty tomato tapenade lends a fresh compliment to the firm, white halibut steaks.

1½ lbs.	fresh or frozen, thawed halibut steaks (or any other firm white fish)
½ tsp.	salt
½ tsp.	freshly ground black pepper
¼ cup	fresh lime juice
2 medium	ripe, tomatoes, chopped
1 tsp.	lemon zest, grated
2 Tbs.	fresh basil, chopped
2 Tbs.	fresh Italian parsley, minced
1 Tbs.	extra-virgin olive oil
2 Tbs.	capers, drained
2 cloves	garlic, chopped
	cooking spray

•••*To increase this recipe, double all ingredients and use a
5, 6 or 7-quart Crock-Pot® slow cooker.*

Lightly coat the Crock-Pot® slow cooker with cooking spray. Season the halibut with the salt and pepper, and place in the stoneware. In a small bowl, combine the lime juice, tomatoes, lemon zest, basil, parsley, olive oil, capers and garlic. Pour the sauce over the halibut. Cover; cook on Low 2 to 3 hours. If desired, spoon the tapenade over the steaks before serving.

CALORIES 253, FAT 7g (Sat 1g), CARBOHYDRATE 3g, FIBER 1g,
PROTEIN 42g, SODIUM 309mg, CHOLESTEROL 65mg

HERBED ARTICHOKE CHICKEN

COOK ON LOW
6 TO 8 HOURS

makes 6 servings

Inviting Greek olives and fresh tomatoes make this a colorful entrée.

1½ lbs.	skinless, boneless chicken breasts
14 oz. can	tomatoes, drained and diced
14 oz. can	artichoke hearts in water, drained
1 small	onion, chopped
½ cup	kalamata olives, pitted and sliced
1 cup	nonfat chicken broth
¼ cup	dry white wine
3 Tbs.	quick-cooking tapioca
2 tsp.	curry powder
1 Tbs.	fresh Italian parsley, chopped
1 tsp.	dried sweet basil
1 tsp.	dried thyme leaves
½ tsp.	salt
½ tsp.	freshly ground black pepper

•••*To increase this recipe, double all ingredients and use a*
5, 6 or 7-quart Crock-Pot® slow cooker.

Combine all the ingredients in the Crock-Pot® slow cooker. Mix thoroughly. Cover; cook on Low 6 to 8 hours (or on High for 3½ to 4 hours).

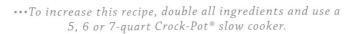

CALORIES 198, FAT 3g (Sat 1g), CARBOHYDRATE 20g, FIBER 0g,
PROTEIN 27g, SODIUM 528mg, CHOLESTEROL 73mg

MEDITERRANEAN TURKEY & TOMATO RICE BAKE

makes 6 servings

Healthy and flavorful, this turkey dish evokes the tastes of the sun-drenched Mediterranean.

2 cups	converted long-grain rice, uncooked
1½ lbs.	skinless turkey breast, cut into bite-sized chunks
2 cups	lowfat, low-sodium chicken broth
¼ cup	Italian parsley, chopped
¼ cup	black olives, sliced
¼ cup	onion, finely chopped
1 clove	garlic, minced
1 tsp.	lemon zest, grated
1 Tbs.	fresh lemon juice
14½ oz. can	stewed tomatoes, undrained
¼ cup	lowfat Parmesan cheese, grated

•••*To increase this recipe, double all ingredients and use a
5, 6 or 7-quart Crock-Pot® slow cooker.*

Combine all the ingredients except the cheese in the Crock-Pot® slow cooker. Mix thoroughly. Cover; cook on Low 6 to 8 hours (or on High for 3 to 4 hours). Sprinkle with Parmesan cheese before serving.

CALORIES 142, FAT 2g (Sat <1g), CARBOHYDRATE 22g, FIBER 1g,
PROTEIN 7g, SODIUM 608mg, CHOLESTEROL 16mg

Easy Chicken Medley

makes 6 servings

Use up those fresh summer vegetables from the farmer's market!

6	skinless, boneless chicken breasts
1 tsp.	salt
1 tsp.	freshly ground black pepper
¼ cup	orange juice concentrate, thawed
1 Tbs.	honey
3 Tbs.	fresh basil, chopped
1 clove	garlic, minced
2	red bell peppers, seeded and chopped
2	zucchini, cut into ¼-inch thick slices
2 cups	fresh pineapple, diced or 14 oz. can pineapple chunks, packed in natural juices, drained

•••*To increase this recipe, double all ingredients and use a 5, 6 or 7-quart Crock-Pot® slow cooker.*

Season the chicken breasts with the salt and pepper and place in the Crock-Pot® slow cooker. In a small bowl, combine the orange juice, honey, basil and garlic. Add the peppers, zucchini and pineapple chunks to the stoneware, and pour the orange juice sauce over all. Cover; cook on Low 6 to 8 hours (or on High for 3 to 4 hours).

CALORIES 293, FAT 12g (Sat 4g), CARBOHYDRATE 19g, FIBER 2g,
PROTEIN 27g, SODIUM 442mg, CHOLESTEROL 99mg

CRAB & SPINACH LASAGNA

makes 8 to 10 servings

Surprisingly low in fat, everyone will love this yummy crab lasagna. Enjoy!

1 large	onion, chopped
2 medium	carrots, diced
2 cloves	garlic, minced
16 oz.	lump crabmeat, shredded, (substitute surimi, if desired)
10 oz. pkg.	frozen chopped spinach, thawed and squeezed dry
1 Tbs.	fresh oregano, minced
2 Tbs.	fresh Italian parsley, minced
1 Tbs.	fresh thyme, minced
1 tsp.	salt
1 tsp.	freshly ground black pepper
10 oz. pkg.	broad lasagna noodles, cooked al denté, drained and cut into thirds

White Sauce:

2 Tbs.	margarine, melted
2 Tbs.	all-purpose flour
1 tsp.	salt
1 cup	nonfat milk
2 cups	lowfat mozzarella cheese, shredded, divided
12 oz. carton	nonfat cottage cheese

•••*To increase this recipe, double all the lasagna ingredients.*
Increase the white sauce ingredients by one-half. Use a 5, 6 or 7-quart Crock-Pot® slow cooker.

In a medium skillet, sauté the onion, carrots and garlic until tender. Add the crabmeat and spinach, and season with the oregano, parsley, thyme, salt and pepper. Transfer the crab mixture to the Crock-Pot® slow cooker. Add the lasagna noodles and mix well to combine.

In a medium mixing bowl, combine the margarine, flour, salt, milk, 1 cup of the mozzarella cheese, and the cottage cheese. Stir and blend for 2 minutes. Pour the white sauce over the lasagna in the stoneware. Cover; cook on Low 4 to 6 hours (or on High for 2 to 3 hours). Thirty minutes before the end of cooking, top the lasagna with the remaining mozzarella cheese and turn to High.

CALORIES 260, FAT 10g (Sat 4g), CARBOHYDRATE 16g, FIBER 0g,
PROTEIN 23g, SODIUM 1198mg, CHOLESTEROL 53mg

Tri-Pepper Southwestern Penne

COOK ON LOW
4 TO 6 HOURS

makes 8 servings

A lively and colorful presentation of vegetables, herbs and pasta!

1 large	onion, chopped
2 cloves	garlic, minced
8	button mushrooms, sliced
1 tsp.	dried oregano
1 tsp.	dried thyme
1 tsp.	dried sweet basil
1 tsp.	dried parsley
1 medium	red bell pepper, sliced
1 medium	yellow bell pepper, sliced
1 medium	green bell pepper, sliced
1 tsp.	salt
1 tsp.	freshly ground black pepper
14½ oz. can	stewed tomatoes, chopped
8 oz. can	tomato sauce
1 cup	water
2 tsp.	granulated sugar
2 Tbs.	dry white wine
1 cup	frozen or fresh kernel corn
4 oz. can	sliced black olives
1 lb.	penne pasta, cooked al denté and drained

•••*To increase this recipe, double all ingredients and use a*
5, 6 or 7-quart Crock-Pot® slow cooker.

In a medium skillet, sauté the onion, garlic and mushrooms until soft. Add the oregano, thyme, sweet basil and parsley. Transfer the vegetables and herbs to the Crock-Pot® slow cooker. Add the remaining ingredients, except for the pasta, and mix thoroughly to combine. Cover; cook on Low 4 to 6 hours (or on High for 2 to 3 hours). To serve, place pasta on six individual plates and spoon the sauce on top of the pasta.

CALORIES 267, FAT 3g (Sat 0g), CARBOHYDRATE 58g, FIBER 5g,
PROTEIN 2g, SODIUM 672mg, CHOLESTEROL 35mg

COOK ON LOW
8 TO 10 HOURS

COOL CHICKEN CURRY SALAD

makes 4 servings

A summertime hit, this salad is full of lean protein and curry flavor. You can serve this as a stand-alone salad or even between pieces of whole grain bread or in a pita as a delicious sandwich.

3 lbs.	whole broiler/fryer chicken
1 tsp.	salt
½ tsp.	freshly ground black pepper
½ cup	nonfat mayonnaise
½ tsp.	cayenne pepper
2½ Tbs.	curry powder
½ tsp.	garlic powder
½ tsp.	salt
2 Tbs.	Major Grey's™ mango chutney
1 small	green apple, cored and finely chopped
2 ribs	celery, finely sliced
3	green onions, finely sliced
¼ cup	golden raisins (optional)
¼ cup	sliced almonds (optional)

•••*To increase this recipe, double all ingredients and use a
5, 6 or 7-quart Crock-Pot® slow cooker.*

Season the chicken with the salt and pepper and place in the Crock-Pot® slow cooker. Pour ¼ cup water into the stoneware. Cover; cook on Low 8 to 10 hours (or on High for 3½ to 5 hours). Remove the chicken from the stoneware and, when cooled, remove the chicken meat from the bones. Discard the skin and bones and cut the chicken into ½-inch pieces. Combine 3 cups of the chicken with the remaining ingredients. If you prefer, you may add additional nonfat mayonnaise. Serve over butter lettuce leaves.

CALORIES 393, FAT 12g (Sat 2g), CARBOHYDRATE 28g, FIBER 1g,
PROTEIN 35g, SODIUM 1211mg, CHOLESTEROL 101mg

BRAISED WINTER SQUASH

COOK ON LOW
8 TO 10 HOURS

makes 6 to 8 side servings

*The sweet, earthy flavors of squash are accented by the soy sauce and honey in this recipe.
Drizzle the sauce over sticky white rice for another flavorful side dish.*

1 large	acorn or kabocha squash (about 2½ lbs. each)
3 Tbs.	reduced-sodium soy sauce
1 cup	vegetable broth or water
3 Tbs.	honey
3 Tbs.	sake or dry white wine

*•••To increase this recipe, double all ingredients and use a
5, 6 or 7-quart Crock-Pot® slow cooker.*

Cut the squash in half and scoop out and discard the seeds. Cut the squash into 2 to 3-inch pieces. Place in the Crock-Pot® slow cooker. In a small bowl, whisk together the remaining ingredients and pour over the squash. Cover; cook on Low 8 to 10 hours (or on High for 2½ to 4 hours.) Remove the squash from the sauce to serve.

CALORIES 117, FAT 0g (Sat 0g), CARBOHYDRATE 28g, FIBER 6g,
PROTEIN 2g, SODIUM 418mg, CHOLESTEROL 0mg

COOK ON LOW
8 TO 10 HOURS

CITRUS BEEF STEW

makes 6 servings

The full flavors of beef are brightened by the fresh taste of orange.

1 cup	onion, finely chopped
1 cup	carrots, finely chopped
1 cup	celery, finely chopped
2 Tbs.	tomato paste
1 cup	nonfat beef broth
¼ cup	fresh Italian parsley, chopped
½ cup	red wine
½ cup	orange juice
3 strips	orange zest
1½ lbs.	beef chuck, cut into 1½-inch cubes
1 cup	butternut squash, cut into 1½-inch cubes
1 cup	new potatoes, quartered
1 cup	green beans, trimmed
1 tsp.	salt
½ tsp.	freshly ground black pepper
1	bay leaf

•••*To increase this recipe, double all ingredients and use a*
5, 6 or 7-quart Crock-Pot® slow cooker.

In a large skillet, sauté the onion, carrots and celery until tender. Place in the Crock-Pot® slow cooker. In a small bowl, whisk the tomato paste into the beef broth. Add to the vegetables. Add the remaining ingredients to the stoneware. Cover; cook on Low 8 to 10 hours (or on High for 4 to 5 hours). Remove the bay leaf before serving.

CALORIES 333, FAT 12g (Sat 4g), CARBOHYDRATE 15g, FIBER 2g,
PROTEIN 25g, SODIUM 668mg, CHOLESTEROL 81mg

BLACK BEAN STUFFED PEPPERS

COOK ON LOW
6 TO 8 HOURS

makes 6 servings

Exciting flavors of Mexico! This lowfat, vegetarian entrée is perfect for any day of the week.

1 medium	onion, finely chopped
¼ tsp.	cayenne pepper
¼ tsp.	dried oregano
¼ tsp.	ground cumin
¼ tsp.	chili powder
2 15 oz. cans	black beans, rinsed and drained
6 tall	green bell peppers, seeded and cored
1 cup	reduced-fat Jack cheese, grated
1 cup	prepared tomato salsa
½ cup	fat-free sour cream

•••*To increase this recipe, double all ingredients and use a
5, 6 or 7-quart Crock-Pot® slow cooker.*

In a medium skillet, sauté the onion until golden. Season with the cayenne pepper, oregano, cumin and chili powder. In a medium mixing bowl, mash half of the black beans with the sautéed onions. Mix in the remaining beans. Place the bell peppers upright in the Crock-Pot® slow cooker, and spoon the black bean mixture into the bell peppers. Sprinkle the cheese over the peppers. Pour the salsa over the cheese. Cover; cook on Low 6 to 8 hours (or on High for 3 to 4 hours). Serve each pepper with a dollop of sour cream.

CALORIES 269, FAT 5g (Sat 3g), CARBOHYDRATE 39g, FIBER 13g,
PROTEIN 17g, SODIUM 413mg, CHOLESTEROL 16mg

CHINESE HOT POT

makes 4 servings

A savory Chinese soup chock-full of fresh, tasty ingredients.

½ lb.	stew beef, cut into chunks
2 medium	zucchini, sliced
8	button mushrooms, cut in half
1 cup	broccoli flowerets
1 cup	extra-firm tofu, cut into cubes
3 cups	vegetable broth
3 cloves	garlic, minced
1 Tbs.	fresh ginger, grated
3 Tbs.	low-sodium soy sauce
1 tsp.	red pepper flakes
1 tsp.	sesame oil
1 Tbs.	honey
½ cup	bean sprouts
½ cup	sugar snap peas, trimmed
4 oz. can	sliced water chestnuts, drained

•••*To increase this recipe, double all ingredients and use a
5, 6 or 7-quart Crock-Pot® slow cooker.*

In the Crock-Pot® slow cooker, combine all the ingredients except for the bean sprouts, snap peas and water chestnuts. Mix thoroughly. Cover; cook on Low 6 to 8 hours (or on High for 3 to 4 hours). Thirty minutes before the end of cooking, add the bean sprouts, snap peas, and water chestnuts and continue cooking until heated through.

CALORIES 262, FAT 6g (Sat 5g), CARBOHYDRATE 21g, FIBER 4g,
PROTEIN 24g, SODIUM 427mg, CHOLESTEROL 42mg

TUSCAN VEGETABLE TORTE

COOK ON LOW
8 TO 10 HOURS

makes 6 servings

Italy offers the best of her bounty in this delicious entrée.

3 medium	potatoes, sliced
1 medium	onion, sliced
2 medium	carrots, sliced on the bias
1	red bell pepper, seeded and sliced into rings
1 medium	zucchini, sliced on the bias
1 cup	fresh or frozen kernel corn
1 cup	skim mozzarella cheese, shredded
2 cups	tomato sauce
1 Tbs.	soy sauce
1 Tbs.	fresh Italian parsley, minced
1 Tbs.	fresh thyme leaves, minced
1 Tbs.	fresh basil leaves, chopped
1 tsp.	salt
½ tsp.	freshly ground black pepper
½ tsp.	ground cinnamon
	cooking spray

•••*To increase this recipe, double all the ingredients except for the sauce ingredients.
Increase the sauce ingredients by one-half. Use a 5, 6 or 7-quart Crock-Pot® slow cooker.*

Coat the Crock-Pot® slow cooker with cooking spray. Layer the vegetables in the order given, sprinkling a little of the mozzarella cheese between each layer. In a medium mixing bowl, combine the tomato sauce, soy sauce, parsley, thyme, basil, salt, pepper and cinnamon. Pour the sauce over the layered vegetables. Top with any remaining mozzarella cheese. Cover; cook on Low 8 to 10 hours (or on High for 4 to 5 hours).

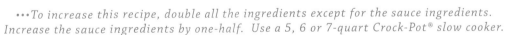

CALORIES 160, FAT 0g (Sat 0g), CARBOHYDRATE 40g, FIBER 6g,
PROTEIN 3g, SODIUM 1082mg, CHOLESTEROL 0mg

COOK ON LOW
6 TO 8 HOURS

TOMATO & BASIL ZITI
WITH ROASTED VEGETABLES

makes 6 servings

The classic summertime combination of tomato and basil complement the vegetables and pasta in this easy entrée.

1 medium	red onion, roughly chopped
1	yellow bell pepper, seeded and chopped
1 medium	carrot, julienned
1 cup	prepared tomato and basil pasta sauce
10 oz. pkg.	frozen spinach, defrosted and drained
14 oz. can	tomatoes, undrained and crushed
8 oz. can	tomato sauce
1	shallot, minced
2 cloves	garlic, minced
½ tsp.	crushed red pepper
1 tsp.	salt
½ tsp.	freshly ground black pepper
½ tsp.	sugar
½ tsp.	ground thyme
½ tsp.	ground sage
3 Tbs.	fresh Italian parsley, chopped
1 cup	lowfat mozzarella cheese, grated
16 oz.	ziti pasta, cooked al denté and drained

•••*To increase this recipe, double all ingredients and use a
5, 6 or 7-quart Crock-Pot® slow cooker.*

Combine all of the ingredients, except for the mozzarella cheese and pasta, in the Crock-Pot® slow cooker. Cover; cook on Low 6 to 8 hours (or on High for 3 to 4 hours). For each individual serving, place a serving of the pasta, sprinkled with the mozzarella cheese, in a pasta bowl, and then ladle the pasta sauce over the top.

**CALORIES 351, FAT 7g (Sat 4g), CARBOHYDRATE 54g, FIBER 4g,
PROTEIN 15g, SODIUM 860mg, CHOLESTEROL 34mg**

Asian Lettuce Wraps

makes 7 servings

This flavorful lowfat dish can be served as an appealing appetizer or a refreshing main course.

1½ lbs.	extra-lean ground chicken or turkey
1 medium	onion, finely chopped
2 ribs	celery, chopped
½ cup	hoisin sauce
3 Tbs.	soy sauce
2 cloves	garlic, minced
2 Tbs.	fresh ginger, grated
1 Tbs.	brown sugar
1 Tbs.	sesame oil
½ Tbs.	Asian chile paste
5 oz. can	bamboo shoots, drained
2 6 oz. cans	sliced water chestnuts, drained, and finely chopped
1 cup	fresh bean sprouts
4	green onions, finely sliced
¼ cup	fresh cilantro, minced
14	crisp iceberg lettuce leaves
¼ cup	hoisin sauce

•••*To increase this recipe, double all ingredients and use a*
5, 6 or 7-quart Crock-Pot® slow cooker.

In the Crock-Pot® slow cooker, combine the chicken, onion, celery, hoisin sauce, soy sauce, garlic, ginger, brown sugar, sesame oil, chile paste, bamboo shoots and water chestnuts. Cover; cook on Low 6 to 8 hours (or on High for 3 to 4 hours). Thirty minutes before the end of cooking, add the bean sprouts, green onions and cilantro. Stir and continue cooking. To serve, place 2 tablespoons of the chicken mixture on an iceberg lettuce leaf and drizzle with hoisin sauce. Roll the filled lettuce leaf into a pocket-style sandwich.

CALORIES 253, FAT 10g (Sat 3g), CARBOHYDRATE 13g, FIBER 0g,
PROTEIN 16g, SODIUM 614mg, CHOLESTEROL 76mg

OATMEAL WITH BERRY MEDLEY

makes 6 servings

Want oatmeal in the morning but don't have the time to make it? Throw these ingredients into your Crock-Pot® slow cooker the night before and wake up to a quick and easy breakfast that is oh-so-tasty and good for you too!

3 cups	old-fashioned, steel cut oats
2½ cups	water
3 cups	apple juice
1 cup	frozen mixed berries, such as strawberries, blueberries, and blackberries
2 Tbs.	brown sugar
¼ tsp.	salt
	cooking spray

•••*To increase this recipe, double all ingredients and use a
5, 6 or 7-quart Crock-Pot® slow cooker.*

Lightly coat the Crock-Pot® slow cooker with cooking spray. Place all of the ingredients in the stoneware and mix to combine well. Cover; cook on Low 8 to 10 hours (or on High 4 to 5 hours).

CALORIES 238, FAT 3g (Sat <1g), CARBOHYDRATE 50g, FIBER 5g,
PROTEIN 6g, SODIUM 102mg, CHOLESTEROL 0mg

CHAPTER NINE

Delectable Desserts & Treats

Arborio Rice Pudding

makes 4 servings

Cook on Low
6 to 8 hours

Creamy and unctuous, this rice pudding is so simple to make and always a crowd pleaser.
Serve with sliced strawberries or raspberries for a fresh flavor.

1	vanilla bean, split
½ cup	arborio rice
3 cups	milk
1 cup	heavy cream
¼ cup	sugar

Scrape out the seeds of the vanilla bean and place the seeds and the bean with the remaining ingredients in the Crock-Pot® slow cooker. Mix to combine well. Cover; cook on Low 6 to 8 hours (or on High 3 to 4 hours). Remove the bean before serving.

COOK ON LOW
4 HOURS

BERRY SAUCE

makes 8 to 10 servings

This versatile sauce can be used in all sorts of ways: on crepes, on waffles, over ice cream, or with pound cake.

6 cups	frozen berries of your choice
	(such as strawberries, blueberries, blackberries)
½ cup	sugar
2 Tbs.	quick-cooking tapioca

•••*To increase this recipe, double all ingredients and use a
5, 6 or 7-quart Crock-Pot® slow cooker.*

Combine all of the ingredients in the Crock-Pot® slow cooker. Cover; cook on Low 4 hours (or on High 2 hours), stirring occasionally.

SUGARED & SPICED PECANS

makes 10 servings

COOK ON HIGH 10
MINUTES & LOW
2 HOURS

Richly glazed pecans are drenched in sweet and savory spices.

1 lb.	pecan halves
½ cup	unsalted butter, melted
½ cup	powdered sugar
1¼ tsp.	ground cinnamon
½ tsp.	kosher salt
¼ tsp.	ground ginger
¼ tsp.	ground allspice
¼ tsp.	ground coriander
¼ tsp.	ground cardamom
	cooking spray

•••*To increase this recipe, double the ingredients and use the 5, 6 or 7-quart Crock-Pot® slow cooker.*

Lightly coat the stoneware with cooking spray. Place the pecans in the Crock-Pot® slow cooker and add the butter and sugar, stirring until the pecans are well-coated. Cover; cook on High for 10 minutes. Reduce to Low and cook for 2 hours, or until the pecans are well-glazed. Just before serving, toss the pecans with the seasonings. Serve while warm.

Classic Baked Apples

Cook on Low
7 to 9 Hours

makes 6 servings

This traditional dish is incredibly simple to prepare.

2 Tbs.	golden raisins
¼ cup	brown sugar
1 tsp.	lemon zest, grated
6 small to medium	baking apples, washed and cored
1 tsp.	ground cinnamon
2 Tbs.	butter
¼ cup	orange juice
¼ cup	water
	whipped cream for garnish

•••*To increase this recipe, double all ingredients and use a
5, 6 or 7-quart Crock-Pot® slow cooker.*

Mix the raisins, sugar and lemon zest and fill the cored center of each apple. Put the apples, standing upright, in the Crock-Pot® slow cooker. Sprinkle with the cinnamon and dot with the butter. Add the orange juice and water. Cover; cook on Low 7 to 9 hours (or on High for 2½ to 3½ hours). Serve with a dollop of whipped cream.

COOK ON LOW
4 TO 6 HOURS

CINNAMON GINGER POACHED PEARS

makes 6 servings

Sweet pears and ginger and cinnamon!. Serve with ice cream or crème fraîche for the ultimate indulgence.

3 cups	water
1 cup	granulated sugar
10 slices	fresh ginger
2 whole	cinnamon sticks
6	Bosc or Anjou pears, peeled and cored
1 Tbs.	candied ginger, minced, for garnish

In the Crock-Pot® slow cooker, combine the water, sugar, fresh ginger and cinnamon sticks. Place the pears upright in the sauce mixture. Cover; cook on Low 4 to 6 hours (or on High for 1½ to 2 hours). Remove the pears from the sauce and let cool. Turn the Crock-Pot® slow cooker to High and heat, uncovered, for about 30 minutes to allow the liquid to reduce to a thick syrup. Drizzle the syrup over the pears and garnish with the candied ginger.

Basil & Cinnamon Syrup Nectarines

Cook on High
2 to 3 hours

makes 8 servings

With a hint of basil, these nectarines are sophisticated enough to serve to the most discerning guests. You can also substitute peaches for the nectarines.

1½ cups	water
3 Tbs.	sugar
½ cup	fresh basil, finely shredded
1	cinnamon stick
8	fresh nectarines, pitted and cut in quarters
1 Tbs.	fresh lemon juice

•••*To increase this recipe, double all ingredients and use a
5, 6 or 7-quart Crock-Pot® slow cooker.*

Combine all ingredients, except the lemon juice, in the Crock-Pot® slow cooker. Cook on High 2 to 3 hours. Remove the nectarines from the syrup and set aside. Let the syrup cool and then strain. Stir the lemon juice into the syrup. Put the nectarines back into the syrup and serve as a topping over your favorite cake or ice cream.

CHOCOLATE COFFEE BREAD PUDDING

makes 6 servings

Chocolate and coffee bring out the best in each other. Top this pudding with a scoop of ice cream, dusted with cocoa powder, for an extra flourish.

1 cup	butter
¼ cup	sugar
1 tsp.	ground cinnamon
4	eggs
1½ cups	chocolate milk
¼ cup	strong coffee
½ cup	currants
½ cup	raisins
½ cup	milk chocolate chips
1 cup	toasted pecans, chopped
4 cups	stale white bread, cut into bite-sized pieces

•••*To increase this recipe, double all ingredients and use a
5, 6 or 7-quart Crock-Pot® slow cooker.*

In a bowl, beat the butter, sugar and cinnamon with an electric mixer. Add the eggs and beat until fluffy. Mix in the chocolate milk, coffee, currants and raisins. Fold the chocolate chips, pecans and bread cubes into the mixture. Pour into a lightly greased Crock-Pot® slow cooker. Cover; cook on Low for 5 to 6 hours (or on High for 2½ to 3 hours).

PEAR AND APPLE CRUNCH COBBLER

COOK ON LOW
8 TO 10 HOURS

makes 6 servings

Capture the warmth of Fall in this fresh cobbler recipe!

3 medium	cooking apples, peeled, cored and roughly chopped
3 medium	pears, peeled, cored and roughly chopped
¼ cup	dark brown sugar, packed
1 Tbs.	flour
1 tsp.	grated lemon zest
1 tsp.	fresh squeezed lemon juice
¼ tsp.	kosher salt
¼ cup	honey
2 Tbs.	unsalted butter, melted
1 tsp.	ground cinnamon
2 cups	prepared granola

•••*To increase this recipe, double all ingredients and use a
5, 6 or 7-quart Crock-Pot® slow cooker.*

Place the apples, pears, brown sugar, flour, lemon zest, lemon juice, and salt in the Crock-Pot® slow cooker, mixing to combine. In a small bowl, combine the honey, butter, cinnamon, and granola. Scatter the granola mixture over the fruit and spices. Cover; Cook on Low 8 to 10 hours (or on High 4 to 5 hours).

COOK ON HIGH
2 TO 3 HOURS

CRANBERRY ORANGE SAUCE

makes about 5 cups

A delicious sauce that successfully pairs cranberry and orange flavors.
Serve as a tangy dessert sauce for your Thanksgiving meal.

4 cups	fresh cranberries
1 cup	sugar
¼ cup	orange juice
¼ cup	water
1 Tbs.	orange zest

Place all of the ingredients in the Crock-Pot® slow cooker and mix to combine. Cover; Cook on High for 2 to 3 hours. Remove the cover and let rest until the sauce reaches room temperature and thickens. Serve chilled or at room temperature.

Chunky Homemade Applesauce

makes about 6 cups

The long, low heat cooking process lends itself well to wonderfully rich fruit sauces. This applesauce has very little sugar so the fruit flavor really shines through.

Cook on Low
8 to 10 Hours

8-10 large	cooking apples (such as Granny Smith), peeled and cored
¾ cup	sugar
½ cup	water
1½ tsp.	ground cinnamon

Chop the apples into chunks. Combine with all of the ingredients in the Crock-Pot® slow cooker. Cover; cook on Low for 8 to 10 hours (or on High 4 to 5 hours). Mash with a potato masher to reach the consistency you prefer.

COOK ON LOW
4 TO 6 HOURS

HONEYED FRUIT COMPOTE

makes about 5 cups

When fresh fruit is not in season, but you're craving a sweet fruit dessert, this compote comes to the rescue.
Serve over slices of angel food cake.

8 oz.	dried figs
8 oz.	dried apricot halves
2 14 oz. cans	sliced peaches, in juice
1½ cups	water
½ cup	sugar
¼ cup	honey
2 Tbs.	lemon juice
1 tsp.	lemon zest

Place the dried fruit and peaches in the Crock-Pot® slow cooker. In a small bowl, whisk together the water, sugar, honey, lemon juice, and lemon zest. Pour the sauce over the fruit. Cover; Cook on Low 4 to 6 hours (or on High 2 to 3 hours).

Sweet & Spicy Mango Pineapple Chutney

Cook on Low
8 to 10 hours

makes about 6 cups

Chutney is an accompaniment to many Indian dishes, but its sweet and spicy nature also lends itself well to other uses. Try it with mayonnaise in your favorite sandwich or wrap, or serve with cream cheese and crackers.

3 large	mangoes, peeled and finely chopped
14 oz. can	pineapple chunks, drained
1 cup	golden raisins
1 cup	light brown sugar
1 cup	red onion, finely chopped
½ cup	cider vinegar
1 clove	garlic, minced
1 medium	hot red pepper, seeded and finely chopped
2 Tbs.	crystallized ginger, minced

•••*Note: This chutney can be processed and stored in canning jars according to standard canning procedures.*

Place all of the ingredients in the Crock-Pot® slow cooker and mix well to combine. Cover; Cook on Low 8 to 10 hours (or on High 4 to 5 hours). Remove the cover and let rest until it reaches room temperature and thickens.

HOMESTYLE TAPIOCA PUDDING

makes 4 servings

A wonderfully creamy and sweet tapioca – everything you remember in a tapioca pudding!
Check the package directions of the tapioca to see if you need to soak the pearls overnight.

4 cups	whole milk
½ cup large	pearl tapioca (soaked per package directions if needed)
½ tsp.	vanilla extract
⅛ tsp.	salt
⅔ cup	sugar
1	egg yolk
2 cups	prepared whipped topping

Place the milk, tapioca, vanilla extract and salt in the Crock-Pot® slow cooker and mix well to blend. Cover; Cook on High 2 hours. In a small bowl, whisk together the sugar and egg yolk. Add small amounts of the cooked tapioca into the egg mixture, whisking to combine until tempered, about 1 cup. Add the egg mixture to the remaining tapioca and stir again. Cook on High for 20 minutes. Transfer the pudding to a medium bowl and cool to room temperature. Cover and chill. Top with the whipped topping to serve.

PEACH AND BLACKBERRY COBBLER

COOK ON LOW
4 TO 6 HOURS
AND HIGH
1 HOUR

makes 6 to 8 servings

Fresh fruit goodness abounds in this easy cobbler. Use summer fruit at its peak or substitute whatever fruit is most fresh from your farmer's market.

2 cups	blackberries
2 cups	peaches, peeled and chopped
½ cup	sugar
2 tsp.	cornstarch
¼ cup	water
1 tsp.	lemon juice
1 cup	all-purpose baking mix
2½ Tbs.	sugar
½ cup	whole milk
½ tsp.	ground cinnamon

Place the blackberries, peaches, sugar, cornstarch, water, and lemon juice in the Crock-Pot® slow cooker. Mix to combine. Cover; cook on Low 4 to 6 hours (or on High 2 to 3 hours). In a small bowl, combine the remaining ingredients until the dough just comes together. Drop 6 spoonfuls of the dough over the fruit. Cover; Cook on High for 1 hour.

COOK ON HIGH
3 HOURS

COCONUT BREAD PUDDING

makes 6 to 8 servings

A twist on the old favorite, this dessert injects the sweet flavor of coconut and golden raisins into the otherwise traditional bread pudding.

1 cup	unsweetened coconut milk
½ cup	milk
1 cup	evaporated milk (substitute light evaporated milk)
4 cups	dry French bread with crust, cut into 1-inch cubes
2 large	eggs
½ cup	sugar
½ tsp.	salt
1½ tsp.	pure vanilla extract
½ cup	sweetened coconut flakes, firmly packed
½ cup	golden raisins

•••*To increase this recipe, double all ingredients and use a
5, 6 or 7-quart Crock-Pot® slow cooker.*

In a lightly greased Crock-Pot® slow cooker, combine the coconut milk, milk, evaporated milk and French bread pieces. Stir thoroughly to mix. In small mixing bowl, beat the eggs, sugar, salt and vanilla extract. Add the egg mixture to the bread and milk mixture in the stoneware. Stir in the coconut flakes and raisins. Cover; cook on High for 3 hours. Serve warm or chilled. Garnish with additional coconut flakes, if desired.

STRAWBERRY & RHUBARB PANDOWDY

COOK ON LOW
6 TO 8 HOURS

makes 4 servings

The tartness of rhubarb accents the sweetness of strawberries in this scrumptious pandowdy.

Filling ingredients:

1½ lbs.	fresh rhubarb, diced into ½-inch pieces
1 pint	strawberries, quartered
1 cup	granulated sugar
1 Tbs.	fresh lemon juice
2 tsp.	lemon zest, grated

Topping ingredients:

¾ cup	all-purpose baking mix
½ cup	unsalted butter
¼ cup	dark brown sugar, packed
	cooking spray

•••*To increase this recipe, double all ingredients and use a
5, 6 or 7-quart Crock-Pot® slow cooker.*

Lightly coat the Crock-Pot® slow cooker with cooking spray. In large mixing bowl, combine the fruit, granulated sugar, lemon juice and lemon zest. Pour into the stoneware. In a separate bowl, combine the baking mix, butter and brown sugar until a crumbly dough is formed. Sprinkle the dough over the fruit mixture, distributing evenly. Cover and cook on Low 6 to 8 hours (or on High for 3 to 4 hours). Serve warm, topped with your favorite ice cream, if desired.

COOK ON LOW
1 TO 2 HOURS

CANDIED BANANAS FOSTER

makes 6 servings

Sure to be a family favorite, a show-stopping dessert doesn't get any easier than this!

6	firm bananas, peeled and cut in quarters
½ cup	flaked coconut
½ tsp.	ground cinnamon
¼ tsp.	salt
½ cup	dark corn syrup
⅓ cup	unsalted butter, melted
1 tsp.	lemon zest, grated
3 Tbs.	lemon juice
1 tsp.	rum
¼ cup	walnuts, chopped
1 qt.	French vanilla ice cream, softened

•••*To increase this recipe, double all ingredients and use a
5, 6 or 7-quart Crock-Pot® slow cooker.*

Combine the bananas and coconut in the Crock-Pot® slow cooker. In a medium mixing bowl, combine the cinnamon, salt, corn syrup, butter, lemon zest, lemon juice, rum and walnuts. Pour over the banana and coconut mixture. Cover; cook on Low 1 to 2 hours. To serve, ladle the bananas and sauce over individual servings of ice cream.

Brownie Bottoms

makes 6 servings

Cook on High
1½ Hours

Warm and gooey, these brownies capture the delight of everyone!

½ cup	dark brown sugar, packed
¾ cup	water
2 Tbs.	cocoa powder
2½ cups	packaged brownie mix
2¾ oz. pkg.	instant chocolate pudding mix
½ cup	milk chocolate chip morsels
2	eggs
3 Tbs.	butter or margarine, melted
½ cup	water
	cooking spray

•••*To increase this recipe, double all ingredients and use a
5, 6 or 7-quart Crock-Pot® slow cooker.*

Lightly coat the Crock-Pot® slow cooker with cooking spray. In a small saucepan, combine the brown sugar, ¾ cup water and cocoa powder and bring to a boil, stirring often. In a large bowl, combine the remaining ingredients to form a thick batter. Spread the batter into the stoneware and pour the boiling mixture over the batter. Do not stir or combine. Cover; cook on High for 1½ hours. Turn to Off and let stand for 30 minutes. Serve while warm, spooning the brownie bottoms over ice cream, fruit or cake.

INDEX